Strolling Down A Shady Lane

Stan Lane

STAN LANE

YouByYou Books

First published in Great Britain by YouByYou Books 2006

ISBN: 0 9550235 1 3

A donation from the sale of this book will be made to the Royal Agricultural Benevolent Institution

Back cover picture Patrick Sutherland. From *Kent* by Nigel Nicolson, 1988. ©Weidenfeld&Nicolson
Set in Times New Roman 11pt
Printed by The Friary Press, Dorchester

YouByYou Books,
Swallow Court,
Dashmonden Lane,
Biddenden,
Kent TN27 8BD.
Tel: 01580 291965
Email: info@youbyyou.co.uk
Website: *www.youbyyou.co.uk*

Contents

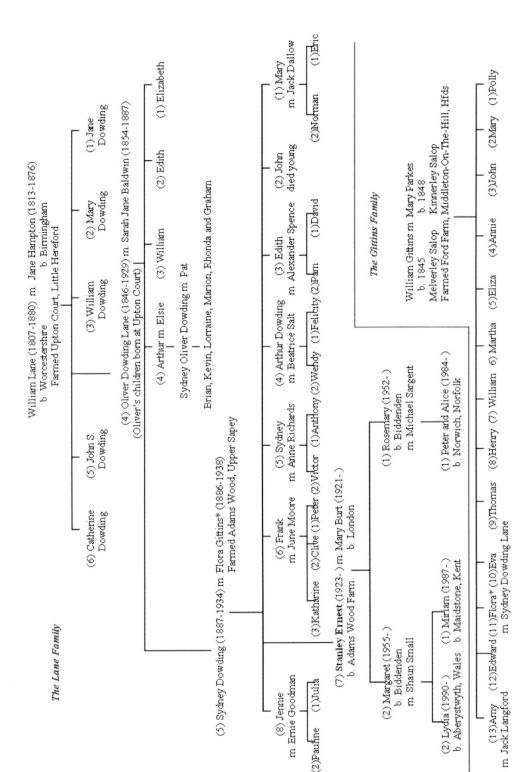

The Lane Family

William Lane (1807-1880) m. Jane Hampton (1813-1876)
b. Worcestershire b. Birmingham
Farmed Upton Court, Little Hereford

(6) Catherine Dowding

(5) John S. Dowding

(3) William Dowding

(2) Mary Dowding

(1) Jane Dowding

(4) Oliver Dowding Lane (1846-1929) m. Sarah Jane Baldwin (1854-1887)
(Oliver's children born at Upton Court)

(4) Arthur m. Elsie   (3) William   (2) Edith   (1) Elizabeth

Sydney Oliver Dowding m. Pat

Brian, Kevin, Lorraine, Marion, Rhonda and Graham

(4) Arthur Dowding m. Beatrice Salt

(3) Edith m. Alexander Spence

(2) John died young

(1) Mary m. Jack Dallow

(1)Felicity (2)Pam   (1)David   (2)Norman   (1)Eric

(5) Sydney Dowding (1887-1934) m. Flora Gittins* (1886-1938)
Farmed Adams Wood, Upper Sapey

(8) Jennie m. Ernie Goodman

(6) Frank m. June Moore

(5) Sydney m. Anne Richards

(1)Julia   (2)Pauline   (3)Katharine   (1)Peter (2)Clive   (1)Anthony (2)Victor

(7) **Stanley Ernest** (1923-) m. Mary Burt (1921-)
b. Adams Wood Farm   b. London

(2) Margaret (1955-)
b. Biddenden
m. Shaun Small

(1) Rosemary (1952-)
b. Biddenden
m. Michael Sargent

(2) Lydia (1990-)
b. Aberystwyth, Wales

(1) Miriam (1987-)
b. Maidstone, Kent

(1) Peter and Alice (1984-)
b. Norwich, Norfolk

(13) Amy   (12) Edward (11) Flora* (10) Eva   (9) Thomas   (8) Henry (7) William 6) Martha   (5) Eliza   (4) Annie   (3) John   (2) Mary   (1) Polly
m. Jack Langford   m. Sydney Dowding Lane

The Gittins Family

William Gittins m. Mary Parkes
b. 1845   b. 1848
Melverley Salop   Kinnerley Salop
Farmed Ford Farm, Middleton-On-The-Hill, Hfds

Introduction

In my early days at school and my teenage years the reading of books was not one of my priorities in life. Being one of the youngest members of the family I failed to follow in the wake of my elder brothers and sisters and recognise the importance of the knowledge to be gained from reading.

As the years passed by I gradually became aware of the enjoyment that I derived from books and told myself that one day I would make an effort to write a story of my own life. Being a little slow in my way of life it took nearly 50 years before I made time to get started but, once begun, I have enjoyed every bit of it. It has taken about 10 years of my spare time in composing it and, I must say, that at times I have got a little confused in what I have written. I have, however, got a great deal of pleasure going back through the pages and wondering how I have managed to recall so many episodes in my life. There must be many happenings that I have failed to remember or succeeded in forgetting, so sorry.

To my knowledge, none of my grandparents wrote about their lives and that lack of family history has inspired me to dedicate this book to my four grandchildren. Maybe they will have a tale or two to pass onto their grandchildren.

Acknowledgements

Many thanks to my family for the encouragement they have given me in writing this book; to Margaret for helping with some typing; to Rosemary for investigating various family histories in the archives; to Alice for putting the manuscript on disc and to Mary for all her loving help and patience in the script reading. Finally, thank you to Anna Foster for her expertise and patience in editing and producing this book.

1. A Herefordshire Lad

I was born on 14th January 1923, the seventh in a family of eight. William, my eldest brother, died at the age of seven months. At about this time one of Mother's sisters died, leaving three children. Mother took the youngest, Reg Watkins, into our family until he reached 15 years.

My birthplace was at Adams Wood Farm in the parish of Upper Sapey in the county of Herefordshire. It was a 17th century three-storey farmhouse with very few modern conveniences.

When I joined the already large family my parents had used all the male family names, i.e. William John, Arthur Dowding, Sydney Albert and Frank Henry. My sisters, Mary Katharine, Edith Flora and Jennie Patricia, were all given family names. I can remember my parents telling me how they bestowed the name of Stanley Ernest on me. Adams Wood Farm was divided on the county boundary of Herefordshire and Worcestershire, hence two parliamentary constituencies gave each of them a vote in each county, a practice which has long ceased. There was an election in 1923 and Stanley Baldwin, who was later to become Prime Minister, was elected for the Bewdley division of Worcestershire, and Sir Ernest Sheperdson for the Leominster division of Herefordshire, so that is how I acquired my name.

Some of my early memories are of the large kitchen table with Mother sitting at the foot and Father at the head, with four children each side. Food has always played an important part in my life, so please bear with me if I mention it from time to time. Father was always strict on punctuality and we all had to be seated before any of us were allowed to start eating. Needless to say, I was mostly well in front, urging my youngest sister Jennie to get seated by my side, the reason being that from time to time she would pass me a few tasty morsels from her plate which I consumed with relish. The high chair that she occupied at the table had been used by all members of the family in turn, and I believe is still in the care of one of them.

Mother, assisted by my two elder sisters, Mary and Edith, used to do all of the cooking and serving of the meals which were always good and plentiful, with Father performing the carving. We boys were sometimes roped into helping with the peeling of potatoes and other not too important chores in the kitchen. Above the kitchen table was a large wooden rack which would have two, sometimes three, flitches - 'sides' of bacon - awaiting their turn to be admitted to the frying pan. On the wall surrounding the kitchen would hang the same number of hams, all awaiting the same destination.

I seem to remember our standard breakfast consisting of a plate of porridge, a rasher of fat bacon together with a slice of delicious fried bread and, as a special treat on Sundays, this was accompanied by a fried egg. The hams were cut into large joints and boiled, and served with parsley sauce and vegetables from the large kitchen garden, which was a place of work for we boys, with the girls doing their share in the house.

The boys helped with the digging, hoeing and weeding; with the girls getting away with the picking of raspberries, strawberries, gooseberries, and both black and red currants. All these were made into jam or jelly, jar upon jar of it and stored for family use.

I seem to remember when I was quite young Father grubbing up the strawberries, but it was quite a while before my brother Arthur told me why he had taken such a drastic step. Seemingly, when Mother thought it was time to start making jam my sisters had to inform her that the birds had cleared them up - with some help from we kids.

Adams Wood Farm consisted of 125 acres of medium loam red soil. At that time, like most of the farms in that part of Herefordshire, it was a general mixed farm. We had six or seven cows, mostly Shorthorns or Crossbreeds. These were milked by Father and two elder brothers before going to school, and also in the evening.

The milk was put through the cream separator, which I remember was a 'Lister', and it was mounted on an old tree trunk in the back kitchen. This relied entirely on man power - or boy power - to operate it. Being the youngest in the train of operators I was introduced to it at about the age of eight. My brother Frank and I had quite a few arguments about whose turn it was turn the handle on this machine, it was mostly agreed to take it in turns for this task. This arrangement came to an end when Frank won a scholarship to attend Bromyard Grammar School as a boarder, only coming home for weekends. The milk was poured into the large container which was situated at the top of the machine and the turning of the handle 'with both hands' would commence, and a bell would ring continuously until the required speed was reached. The tap was now turned on, allowing the milk to flow down into the machine which separated the cream from the milk. The cream flowed out of the top spout and skimmed milk out of the lower one. This was fed to calves and pigs along with a cereal mix. The cream was stored in china bowls in the adjoining dairy until the day that it was made into butter.

Monday was butter-making day, in readiness to be taken to the produce market at Tenbury Wells on Tuesday. The cream was tipped into the large end over end churn. I remember this as a rather handsome machine with its highly polished oak barrel with two shiny brass screw clips to secure the lid. It stood on four legs and through the centre of it was a large handle. This had to be turned for quite some time before the butter was formed. At sometime during the churning the lid was removed and salt was added, which I rather think was just for flavouring. During the cooler winter months this churning took quite a long time, but with the warmer months of summer the butter came much quicker. When it had formed into a lump it was put into what was called a butter worker, which in turn rid it of the 'butter milk'. The next operation was to pat it into neat half-pound rolls, called Worcestershire Rolls, which was achieved with two wooden butter hands.

On the balance scales that Mother used to weigh these rolls was a very mouldy old penny piece alongside of the weight. I think this was to ensure that good weight was always given. I seem to remember coveting that penny for quite a few years, thinking that it would have been much better placed in my pocket than for it to get more mouldy as time passed!

The calves that were reared on the farm were Hereford crossed with the Shorthorn cows that we kept for milking. None of them were fattened on the farm but were sold to other farmers as stores at about 18 months of age, for further fattening.

Owing to my minority, I wasn't allowed to take part in helping drive the cattle to market. My two elder brothers and cousin Reg always seemed to have tales to tell me of exciting experiences that they encountered on these journeys.

The favourite one was when Father sent them to a small cattle and sheep fair at Clifton-on-Teme, a distance of a couple of miles. They only had three small steers to drive there and all went well until about 150 yards before they got to the fair ground they had to pass the Red Lion pub. Now being a day that the landlord of this establishment would be expecting a boost in the number of farmers and dealers that he would play host to, he had left the front door of the pub open, I think to make it look quite welcoming.

Alas, as these steers got abreast of the open door they thought it had been left open for their benefit, and the leading one of them entered promptly, followed by his two mates. This door opened into the public bar where the cleaning lady was putting the final touches to her morning's work before the first customers were expected. She had her back to the door and as the animals had walked in very stealthily she hadn't heard them enter, but as one of them nudged her 'back end' she let out an enormous shriek and really put fright into these animals. In their desperation to get away from this good lady they managed to knock over her mop bucket and spill the soapy water all over her nice clean floor. By now my two brothers and cousin, aged 15, 14 and 12, had arrived in the bar just in time to see the steers hastily making their retreat through the next door which unfortunately led into the saloon bar. On seeing the boys looking quite upset about this disastrous entry, she told them to "get those bloody animals out in double-quick time". They managed to manoeuvre them through the saloon with only one chair being knocked over. However, the door from this room led into the very clean and tidy kitchen. That was where one of them really disgraced himself, lifting his tail and waving it just as he was discharging a gut full of very grassy dung all over the spotless kitchen floor.

By now the cattle, my two brothers and Reg, had become rather unwelcome guests in this establishment and help was urgently required. This arrived in the form of a very irate landlord, and with the help of his boot and a few choice swear words, they managed to get them out into the back yard and into the fair field which lay at the rear of the pub. When Father arrived by pony and trap at the sale yard he was soon to learn of the trouble that his beasts had caused at the Inn. We never did hear the outcome of Father's visit to offer an apology to the landlord for the damage that these animals had caused, but I am sure it was settled amicably.

The sheep flock at our farm consisted of about 40 breeding ewes. They were mostly of the Clun Forest breed, or their crosses. A Shropshire ram was used to mate these ewes. I believe they produced lambs that were able to grow to good weights at quite an early age and were sold by auction at Tenbury Wells market. The Shropshire breed has fallen out of favour and is now almost confined to the Rare Breeds.

The lambing, or 'yeaning' as it was known in that part of the country, took place in early March. This was a very important time in our year, and still is today, but on a much larger scale. Mostly the ewes yeaned in the old orchard adjoining the farm yard, but if the weather turned cold or wet they were brought into the comfort of the barn. The sight of them lying on a nice bed of golden straw is still vivid in my memory.

Most years we had a few orphan 'tiddling' lambs and feeding them was the job of us younger members of the family. During the first week of this task there was quite a tussle to be up front to start feeding these lambs with milk from the bottle, but after a week or so the novelty began to wear and a bit of chasing was needed to take our place in the three times a day routine. This is a situation that I have seen repeated in more recent times!

When the lambs were about two weeks of age they were tailed, and the male lambs were castrated. This operation was far removed from the easier and more humane rubber ring method which was introduced in the 1950s, and is still in use at the present time. At the exit to the pen Father would sit astride the same bench that was used for the pig killing. Each of us boys would catch a lamb in turn and sit it on the end of the bench facing him. Father took his sharp pocket knife and neatly cut the end off the scrotum and gently drew out the testicles. Then he would cut off the tail with one blow with mallet and chisel and the lamb went free. This job was confined to Saturdays when plenty of help was available. I can never remember any of my sisters witnessing this gruesome operation.

One of the highlights of the summer was the sheep wash day. This also took place on a Saturday early in June in readiness for the shearing which took place about 10 days later. Having no place to wash them at Adams Wood we used to drive them down to Hanley Mill, a distance of about two miles. It was a very quiet road and in the few years that I helped with this job I can't remember ever getting any problems with traffic. The mill was in disuse, but the old water wheel and some of the machinery was still in place and brother Frank and I used to sneak off and explore this old site. The washing was carried out in the mill race which was fed with water from a very picturesque stream. The sheep were slipped into the water, and guided through the brick-lined mill race which was about 30 feet long and five feet wide. As they were swimming they were scrubbed with long-handled, T-shaped wooden tools. After running the gauntlet of three or four men with these scrubbers they walked up the ramp out of the water and back to their lambs, which didn't get washed owing to the fact that they weren't to get shorn. The whole reason for the washing was to clean the wool and make it more presentable to the wool merchants. This washing of sheep is a practice that is rarely carried out these days. The return trip home was much more leisurely as by now the sheep, and us boys, were getting a little weary. Most of the neighbouring farmers used the same facilities that we used, and mostly on the same day. It used to be quite a problem to keep these small flocks of sheep from getting mixed up. After all the years that have passed since those days, I can honestly say that I longed for the excitement of this happening, but alas, it only happened on one occasion in my childhood, though it was worth it to see men, dogs and boys sorting them out.

The shearing was done by Father. He also instructed cousin Reg and brothers Arthur and Syd in the art of shearing. Having only a small flock to shear he had plenty of time to give them careful tuition. The three of them eventually went on to do quite a lot of shearing in their various places of work. It was a good many years before I got the chance to try my hand at it.

Unlike today with the use of electricity, the power to drive these machines was provided by man, and occasionally, boy power! I was allowed to turn the handle sometimes, with the threat of losing my job if I couldn't keep a good regular pace. When this happened, which wasn't too often, one of my brothers took over the task.

In common with nearly all family farms of that time, most species of poultry were kept, with ours being no exception. Mother was in control of all these with the assistance of us boys. About 70 to 80 laying hens were kept. They supplied all the eggs consumed by our large family. The surplus was sold in Tenbury produce market each Tuesday. They were taken along with the butter, and sometimes rabbits and other produce that was available .

This weekly trip to market was always in the trap which was pulled by Kit, the bay mare, who was greatly loved by all the family. Alas, one morning early in 1933, Father went out to the stables to feed the horses, and found Kit lying dead in her loose box. He was very sad about this, as were all of the family. She was 32 years of age. Both Syd and Edith took turns to ride her to follow the Teme Valley Fox Hounds. He had bought her from Uncle Will in 1915. That was the year that Father took over the tenancy of Adams Wood Farm from Uncle Will, who in turn took over the Ford Farm from Grand Father Gittins who then retired.

The laying hens consisted of several breeds, both pure and cross breeds. The ones that seem to have stuck in my mind are Buff Rocks, White Wyndottes, Rhode Island Reds and a sprinkling of White Leghorns. They were housed in a large shed at one end of the farmyard and were allowed out to free range by day. Although there were plenty of nest boxes they seemed to prefer to find all kinds of odd corners in which to lay their eggs. On our return from school each day one of us was detailed to go and collect these eggs that had been laid by these wayward hens. Occasionally, these nests were never found until a hen would be seen strutting along with a brood of chicks in tow. These carefree broods were never frowned on as we needed several each year to keep the numbers up. This was usually achieved by Mother selecting a broody hen and sitting her on 13 eggs. She would put them in a small tin-roofed coop. In the front of these coops were slats of wood which restricted the hen, but let the chicks have their freedom. These coops were put out in the orchard and it was one of us boys who, each evening, had to make sure that the shutters were shut safely to keep out any fox that might be looking for a free takeaway meal.

After three weeks 10 or more chicks would hatch out and remain with the hen for a month or so, and were then transferred into a larger pen for a further four months, and the pullets would then join the laying flock. The cockerels were killed and dressed and sold in the produce market. The old hens usually ended up as boilers and two of them made a meal for the whole family.

There were a small number of bronze turkeys kept with about 15 hens, and one cock strutting around the farmyard. This cock was always treated with great respect as he was rather a frightening-looking bird. Some of the turkey eggs were hatched out on our farm, and the surplus sold as hatching eggs at the market. The poults were reared and fattened for the special dressed poultry sales at Christmas.

Mother used to buy about two dozen goslings each spring. These were reared and fattened, and joined the turkeys at the same Christmas sale. These geese were kept in part of an old cattle shed. Each morning they were turned out and driven to the orchard where they spent the day grazing. Each afternoon they wandered back to the farmyard and spent quite a time on the large pond situated in the centre of the yard.

About an hour before dark they were fed their only meal of the day, and this was always given in their shed with the idea that they would willingly leave the pond and return to feed. The majority of them did just that, but a few of them were rather reluctant to work to rule and stayed on the water.

It was our job to get them off the pond and into their shed. This was achieved by throwing clods at them (we were forbidden to use stones), and we used to get quite accurate at getting our shots just far enough behind them to encourage them on their way. Often slight arguments would arise as to which of us had made the most useful shot to hasten them on their way from the pond.

A couple of large white sows and their progeny were the only pigs that were kept. Most of the piglets were fattened and sold to the butcher at Clifton-on-Teme. The ones that didn't go that way found their selves hanging up as bacon in the farm kitchen, destined for consumption by the family. During the winter months the Pig Killer, as he was known, visited the farm two or three times to kill and dress one of these pigs. Those for home consumption were kept on to a much larger weight than the ones that went to the butcher.

The Pig Killer would arrive in his pony and trap complete with knives, saws, a smart leather apron and a pig bench. On to this bench the pig, with some amount of pushing and heaving, would be placed, laying on its side. Following one bolt shot into its forehead, it died instantly. Then its throat was cut and the blood saved into a large stone (steen) jar, to be used later in the making of black puddings. As soon as the pig was declared dead it was rolled off the bench onto a bed of straw. This was fired, and when the flames had died down the carcass was scraped of all the bristles on its skin. When this operation was completed it was hauled into the barn, and by its hind legs was strung up to a beam. It was then slit open and all of its entrails removed. The heart, liver and flead (fat used for baking) were saved for the making of faggots. These were delicious when cooked and were soon devoured by the family. All the fat was removed from the inside of the carcass and rendered down into lard which in turn got used for cooking. I still consider that the residue of this operation, pork scratching, was the most delicious of all the pig. These very tasty morsels were kept in a large bowl inside the dairy, and we were allowed 'ad lib' access to them on our return home from school. I seem to remember my mouth watering on the final part of the journey, thinking of what was awaiting my immediate attention! Today, the measly things sold in pubs that pass as pork scratchings taste nothing like those of my childhood.

After about four days of hanging, the Pig Killer came back to the farm and cut the carcass into six joints, two hams, two shoulders and two flitches. Father would then lay them out on stone slabs in the farm dairy ready to start the curing of them. I never learned much about this task, but remember him rubbing large amounts of salt into the flesh, and Salt Petre around the bones. After a few weeks of regular turning, the joints were hung up in the kitchen, to await their turn to be consumed by the family.

Having only a couple of sows on the farm didn't warrant keeping a boar of our own, and when one of the sows came into season she was taken to mate with a boar that one of our neighbouring farmers kept with his herd of pigs. This was Mr Churchill's Fall Farm which lay about midway between us and the village school. I remember one morning Father discussing with my two elder brothers the fact that one of our sows was in season and would need to be taken to the boar for mating. The day being Tuesday was just the day Father regularly went to Tenbury market. My brothers suggested that they should take her on the way to school and bring her back on their return home in the afternoon. No way was I going to miss out on this little jaunt and I was allowed to set off with them some time earlier than usual. Looking back, after all the years that have passed since that morning, I think we should have left a good hour sooner!

A long rope had been secured around one hind leg of the Sow, supposedly as a means of security and, as things turned out, it was a life-saver. All went well driving her out of the sty and through the yard but, alas, when she got out into the first meadow she must have thought freedom was the order of the day, and sped off at considerable speed, with my brothers hanging on to the rope for dear life. As I was not yet capable of their superior speed I was soon left trailing behind, shedding a few tears. Eventually I caught up with them, and managed not to be outdone for the rest of the journey. Each fresh meadow that we entered the Sow took off again with us following, sometimes on our feet, but mostly on our backsides. By the time we reached Mr Churchill's farm we were quite puffed out, after trying to restrain a pig weighing 350 pounds. It was then decided that no way were we going to take her back home after school that afternoon. Father and cousin Reg managed to get her home later in the day, with much less stress than the morning's episode.

On being nearly an hour late arriving for school I can still recollect Arthur explaining to Mr Routledge, the school master, the reason for our late coming was due to the misbehaviour of a certain Sow which we had to deliver to the Fall Farm, to make love to Mr Churchill's Boar.

Mr Routledge, who died in 1933, had been the Master of Stanford-on-Teme school for 35 years, and was a much loved and respected man. He understood about farming and all the country ways of both man and beast. On hearing Arthur's explanation of our late arrival, he expressed the hope that this mating would result in a fine litter of piglets being born in the weeks ahead. I just wonder what the present-day teacher would write in the attendance record to account for the one-hour late coming of three pupils.

At this stage in my ramblings, I must apologise for getting too far

15

ahead, or too far behind with my story. Trusting entirely to my memory, which tends to slip, I am finding a few gaps coming to light. One of these concerns my attendance, along with several other members of the family, on most Sunday mornings at Stanford Church. Unlike the clergy of today, the Rector had just one parish to take care of, with the result that he had ample time to make very long drawn-out sermons, before returning to the Rectory with his wife and partaking in a substantial Sunday lunch, prepared and served by the cook and house maid (yes, in those days most of the Clergy seemed able to support a small domestic staff). During these rather prolonged sermons, his wife usually sat in one of the pews close to the pulpit, and most often would bring some knitting which kept her awake for the early part of the service before dropping off into rather a deep slumber! Towards the end of the sermon the Rector sought fit to bring his good lady back to the land of the living. This was achieved with the aid of a few loud coughs which, as they got louder, eventually bore fruit, and enabled him to bring his sermon to a very welcome conclusion.

Occasionally, in the absence of Sam Yeoman, the regular organ blower, I used to take his place, much to the dismay of Miss Scyrme, the organist. Sometimes I got a little confused as to when to start blowing, but with a few waves of her arms and some rather fearsome facial expressions I just about coped.

The reason for Sam's absence was that he had to cycle over to Knightwick Sanatorium to visit his elder brother who was suffering with tuberculosis. Sadly, Bill died at the age of 13 years. During my years at Stanford School three children died from the same disease. That number was out of the whole school, which numbered just 35 pupils.

When I attained the great age of five I was introduced to life at Stanford-On-Teme School and remained there until the age of 12. I was put under the very careful eye of my brother, Arthur, who was seven years my senior. I think he must have been well briefed by my parents regarding my expected misbehaviour! I seem to remember that he had good cause to severely reprimand me on several occasions. One morning father had given him and Syd the job of taking two of our working horses to the blacksmith on their way to school. This was considered a very manly job by the three younger members of the family, and we pestered our two elder brothers to be allowed to have a ride. Eventually, after a lot of whimpering, we were given a leg up and arrived at school, two mounted on one horse and me on the second. The blacksmith's shop was about another half mile beyond the school. After dismounting, the idea was for us to go into the school. Now I had other thoughts and I left the other two, and at a discreet distance, followed the two grooms with their horses on to the smithy. After they were tied up and left with the instruction to have "new shoes all round", they would collect them on their way home from school in the afternoon. When Arthur found me lurking at the back of the smithy he was far from proud of his youngest brother and didn't hesitate to tell him so. You see, unbeknown to me, arrangements had been made for them to be up to half an hour late, to allow them time to walk back to school. Unfortunately, this concession didn't include one six-year-old miserable little brat as part of the operation. This same boy got quite a lengthy reprimand from Miss Whinall, his teacher, for being late.

We used to walk to school - which was a distance of two miles - along a very quiet road. Very little traffic used this road; some days we would see perhaps two vehicles on our way to or from school, and other days none. There was always great excitement at the sight of any approaching vehicle, and lots of hand-waving would be indulged in by our little crowd. In most cases we got a friendly response from the occupants. There was a very steep hill on this road, called Stony Head. One afternoon, as we were on our way home, we spotted some fresh form of activity up at the top of the hill and we all made a great effort to be the first on the scene. On arrival, we found three men spreading grit from the back of a wagon, and a very smoky steam roller was methodically rolling the grit in to the road behind them. Now after we all stood and observed for a while what was being done to disfigure our road, it was decided that some form of protest was called for. After a few ideas, it was suggested by one of the boys that some object should be placed in the road to halt the progress of this beastly steam roller. Being the younger of the boys in the group, I thought now was my chance for me to show them how to go about this operation. I spotted a sizeable lump of rock on the roadside and, with great haste, grabbed it and threw it right under the front of the roller, and it was promptly rolled into the surface, leaving quite an ugly scar on the road. Now seeing what a mess this had made of the road I felt quite elated at my bit of folly.

This feeling only lasted for a very short while, for as I was making my getaway to join the other boys to accept a hero's return, the engine driver had other thoughts. He dismounted from his machine and took chase after me. He was a man with rather a generous waistline and I was sure that I would be able to outrun him, but how wrong I was! He soon caught up with me, grabbed me by the scruff of the neck and, with both his big sooty hands, gave me the blackest face I have ever had. After about three minutes of this facial massage he let me free and, with a well-aimed kick on my backside, dismissed me with the phrase, "That will teach you, you little bugger!"

This bit of advice fell on very fertile, eight-year-old ears. On my arrival home, I had to explain how I came by such a black face. After hearing my story, my parents' sentiments leaned towards the actions of the engine driver.

For much of the way to school the road led through a large forest belonging to the Stanford Court Estate. On our way home, we would explore the woods which were full of all kinds of exciting paths and lots of good trees, just right for climbing, especially the huge beech trees. On one side of the wood there were quite a lot of sweet chestnut and walnut trees. Each autumn we used to make the extra long trek to the area where these trees were situated and fill our satchels with some of the delicious nuts that lay in abundance under the trees. We never got into trouble from the estate workers for helping ourselves to the nuts. I think this exercise had been indulged in by several generations of children before us and had become a part of the school calendar.

There was one area adjoining the road to school, where we were none-too-welcome. This was the orchard which belonged to the Rectory. It was an area of about four acres of mixed cooking, eating and cider apples, pears, cherries, plums and damsons. Now all the children in our little gang would have had the same type of orchard at home, with just the same varieties of fruit as the Rector had in his orchard. In our school days pocket money was something we just heard about but very rarely possessed.

Without the means to buy anything, just an occasional packet of sweets, we got by with an abundance of fruit from these very mixed orchards. There was almost a year-round supply of one kind of fruit or another, either fresh or stored for use during the winter months. Most days we would be able to include some of these goodies in our lunch bags, so there wasn't really any need for us to scrump fruit from the Rector's orchard, but that is what we did quite often! There was one part-time gardener employed at the Rectory but, unfortunately, he used not always to work the same days. This used to cause us quite a bit of bother, as on the days we planned to do a bit of scrumping one or two of us had the task of establishing if he was at work that day. Some days the observers would get it all wrong and would give us the all-clear. On these occasions we would be over the orchard gate, filling our pockets with the forbidden fruit, only to find the gardener looking out for us. He was rather an old and infirm man, and the best he could do was bellow at us with a very loud voice and frighten us on our way back over the gate.

One year there was such an abundance of fruit in the orchard that the Rector came down to the school and announced that the children would be very welcome to go into his orchard and take whatever fruit they liked. He would also leave the gate open and save us the bother of having to climb over it. Now, with this bit of kindness, we all lost our appetites for the Rector's fruit as we knew that it wouldn't taste the same if it hadn't been scrumped. The gardener also seemed a bit disappointed with not having to catch the boys out, as I secretly think he used to enjoy his verbal outrage and see us all scampering back over the gate, mostly retaining some of our ill-gotten gains.

Apart from our farm orchard of mixed fruit we had a small orchard of damsons, also some of the hedge rows had been planted with damson trees at regular spacing. During the month of September all of our family used to have to help pick this fruit. This was also the month that the school was closed for the hop-picking holidays (today's equivalent of summer holidays). The elder members of the family (boys and girls), used to pick the tops of the trees with ladders and the younger ones were only allowed to pick what we could reach from the ground, sometimes with a bit of perseverance we managed to get part way up a ladder. Most years, the crop would amount to between six and 10 tons in total, but one year (1932) we had the record amount of 13 tons. One night, at the end of the season, as we were all sitting down to tea my father announced that as a result of such a fine crop of damsons, having been picked by all the family, there was a little extra money in the bank. Having had requests from my elder sisters and brothers to buy a wireless he now felt that he was able to afford one, and that day had put in an order for a three-valve set and it would be delivered the next week. My most vivid memories of that set are of the supplier coming quite frequently to try and get it to work as it should. He used to get most frustrated when it didn't respond to his tinkerings. He had a very squeaky voice, plus a rather pronounced Adams Apple, which seemed to wobble as his frustration increased. His visits mostly occurred when we were all sitting round the tea table. I am sure we got more entertainment from his antics than ever we got from the wireless set.

The damsons were packed into round, wicker sieves with 28lbs in each one. They were lined with thick blue paper with the top secured with split hazel sticks. Each afternoon, the day's picking was loaded on to the horse dray, taken to Newnam Bridge station and loaded onto a train bound for Manchester. On arrival there they went to a firm by the name of Austin Coe, all to be used for the manufacture of dye. Some days I was allowed to accompany my elder brothers on their journey to and from the station which was about five miles from Adams Wood. I seem to remember that one of the conditions of me being allowed on this journey was that I had been on my best behaviour for that day. I did my best, but slipped up on a few occasions, and had to stay at home and wait for another chance of a ride.

At Stanford School we were not confined to the playground at lunch times. Some days we would go off on a fox and hound trail which was always good fun. The fox was usually selected from one of the elder boys (or girls) and given a few minutes start before the hounds set off. Some of the younger members would start with the rest of the field, but rarely made the full chase, and dropped out to return to school and await the rest of the pack. We used to cover quite a distance over fields and small areas of woodland. The school bell used to be rung 10 minutes before lessons were due to begin so we had no reason to be late back.

One of our other favourite pastimes was jumping the brook. This game had its hazards, as the brook ran from up in the hills above the school and eventually joined the River Teme. We would start our game by trying to make the clearest jump over any given section of the brook. Making our way upstream we would come to either hard or easy jumps. The idea being for the hard ones to be attempted only by the elder boys. This rule was mostly observed, but there came a time when the younger ones thought that they could do as well as their elders. This way of thinking caused me quite a bit of discomfort one day when we were having a very successful session of jumping. One of the older boys dared me to jump a wide and deep section of the brook, which was considered to be the most challenging of all the jumps. I thought, now was the chance for me to prove what I was capable of doing! Making quite a good effort to succeed, I just managed to miss the other side by a few inches and landed in some very cold water right up to my waist. For the rest of the afternoon I had to sit in my wet clothes. I didn't dare to tell the master of my predicament for fear of a severe reprimand for trying to attempt such a task.

Some days, instead of going all the way to school by way of the road we would leave Adams Wood, crossing the fields to the Fall Farm where we joined the Churchill household. They boasted a family of 10 children, seven boys and three girls. In my days all but three of them had

20

left school, the youngest being Freda. She was a semi-cripple and had both her legs in irons. She had a donkey, Dobbin, on which she was carried to and from school. Sometimes I was privileged to sit behind her and travel to school in majestic style. Now, like all donkeys, Dobbin had a will of his own and didn't fail to use it. He wouldn't be hurried and, with the slightest bit of prompting, he would come to a complete stop. After what he considered was a reasonable time of forgiveness he would carry on his way. He had travelled this path for several years and had been relieved of his bridle for some time. He knew his way and wasn't going to be persuaded by a few tugs on his bit to step off this path. The route to school from the Fall Farm took us through a meadow into a forest and out into the road, about a mile in distance. Part way down this path was a stream where a plank had been placed. I am sure Dobbin used to feel very proud of himself as he crossed this plank, it was the only time that he was ever seen to wave his tail.

When the forest path got very wet and the stream was in flood the Churchill children would walk up their long drive and meet us on our road. Now Dobbin didn't care greatly for using the hard road. It may have been the fact that he had no shoes or missed the canopy of trees on his woodland path. He made frequent stops bang in the middle of the road. On arrival at school he would be turned loose in a small paddock where he would stay until he was required for the return journey.

Another reason that the trek to school via the Fall Farm was so attractive was the fact that they always had a barrel of cider on tap. Having walked up through the woods on our way home from school, especially on a hot summer afternoon, this was more than welcome. Mrs Churchill would give the girls a glass of lemonade, but the boys were all considered able to partake in a glass of cider - and on very hot days that got stretched to two! This drink was of a low alcoholic content, hence the freedom with which us kids were allowed to partake in the consumption of it.

All the farms in our area used to make cider. On our own farm there was always an abundance of cider apples and pears. They would be shaken from the trees by Father and us kids would pick them up into sacks for our own use. The surplus was loaded onto wagons and transported to Bulmer's cider factory at Hereford.

The cider press used to go round from farm to farm pulled by horse power. It always seemed to come to our farm on a Saturday, much to our delight, as we all helped in the work of the day. The first operation was to tip the sacks of fruit into the hopper that was on top of the grinder.

This machine was driven by a rather ancient paraffin engine. The crushed fruit was then put into large Hessian mats, the tops of these were folded over the pulp. When the press had about 10 of these mats placed on top of each other the pressing would commence. This operation was carried out by a large screw which was situated in a very stout, timber frame above the press. Two men each took a handle and turned this screw down onto a heavy kind of table which pressed the juice out of the fruit. This turning didn't stop until the juice ceased flowing into the large open tub below and water was then added to the juice. From this tub it was taken across to the cider house and poured into Hogs Heads, oak barrels which when full contained 60 gallons.

I never did find out the ratio of water to juice. Seeing that there was one Hogs Head, kept exclusively for the children, I rather fancy we had a little more water in our brew!

Two important days in our school year were the Church Garden Fete and the Christmas Dinner. The fete used always to take place on the second Wednesday in June, the venue being the huge lawn in the Rectory garden. Beyond a tall yew hedge at the rear of this lawn was the vegetable garden. Now in this area there was a large wired-in section which was planted with raspberries and strawberries. It was the ambition of most of the boys (me being one of them), to gain access to this establishment at least once during the afternoon's festivities. The raspberries were not quite ripe so early in the season, but fortunately the strawberries were delicious! It wasn't always easy to get access to this wired-in garden. The Rector and his gardener were both involved in other activities on the lawn. The Rector would be strutting around talking to his parishioners. The gardener always ran the Bowling-for-a-Pig stall. Occasionally, they would leave their duties and go to have a quick look, to see if the strawberries were in any danger. Mostly the alarm was raised on their approach, and the cage would be cleared of intruders as quick as lightning.

We school children used to take part in quite a few activities during the afternoon. Country dancing was one of the most popular of the shows, and was watched by all the adults, with lots of clapping after each event. One year I was included in the team that danced the Maypole. Why I was picked I will never understand as I had never shown any interest in such a sissy game. Miss Whinal, our teacher, had the eight members of our team practising in the playground, each afternoon for about eight days before the Fete. The dancing of the Maypole should be a fairly easy and delightful spectacle to be admired by all who care to watch it. This wasn't so on that June day all those years ago. I hadn't proved to be the most promising of pupils for the teacher, but she must have thought me just about capable of taking part in the team that she was taking to the Fete. The dance started well, and would have continued so, except that one horrid little boy danced three steps, where only two were required. The result of this faulty step meant that this said boy got his ribbon mixed up with the next dancer. This act caused a lot of confusion within the team. The teacher was standing on the perimeter of the lawn, frantically calling out to me how to get back into my correct position. I tried my best, but to no avail. Things got worse. I felt so sorry for the teacher, and the rest of the team, as the dance came to such a disastrous end. That sad episode confirmed my opinion not to get involved in the dancing of the Maypole ever again.

The Christmas Dinner was always of special interest to we kids. All other school days we took our lunch in our satchels, and ate it in great haste, prior to whatever games we had chosen to partake in for that day.

The Dinner always took place on the day that the school broke up for the holidays. The money that financed this feast, was the result of a legacy, left to the Village School by one of the earlier Lords of the Manor, the Winington family, who were closely related to Sir Winston Churchill's forebears. There not being any cooking facilities at the school, the dinner had to be cooked at the Rectory and transported down to the school. Not much learning was expected of us on this morning. Our time was spent decorating the classroom, with holly and mistletoe, which had been brought in by the children. The classroom had to be arranged with all the desks in a semi-circle facing the front, where two trestle tables had been placed in readiness for the forthcoming Banquet.

This festive day had been celebrated in much the same fashion for many years, bar the occasional mishap. After spending the morning preparing the classroom, we were allowed out into the road to await the arrival of our dinner. When we caught site of a pony and trap coming down the hill, we knew all was well. The pony was led by the gardener, with the Rector and his wife sitting in the trap. Following the trap would be the cook and the house maid from the Rectory. On arrival at school, the procession was met by the Head Master and the Infant Teacher, who helped to carry the various dishes into the classroom. Without fail, the two main dishes contained a very large joint of roast beef. Each of these found the Rector and the Head with their carving knives at the ready. By now, the children would all be sat eagerly waiting for their feast of the year. Very generous slices of roast beef and huge helpings of vegetables were served by the four ladies. Grace was always said by the Rector before battle commenced.

One tradition of this annual celebration was to bring a drinking vessel to school. This was because each year the Rector included a few jars of his own Cider with the other Christmas fare. Now this Cider was usually considered of a very inferior quality to what we were all used to drinking at home. Our glasses, or mugs were each filled, but before the feast was finished, most of this drink had been discreetly consigned to the ink wells which were situated at the front of each desk.

I remember one year, four of us boys were sitting on a front-row desk, about 10 feet in front of the table where the meat was being carved. A vase of mistletoe, with lots of berries, was positioned on our desk and it became pretty obvious that better use could be made of these berries than just leaving them for decorative use. Now the Rector was a large man, with rather a generous stomach, which on this day was covered with a very smart white apron. After a silent discussion among we four boys, it was decided that this apron, would make an excellent target for our missiles. We each took turns to flick one of these berries at the target. Not having had a chance for any practice at this sport, it was after quite a few shots that I became the first one to get a bull's eye. The Rector, who was rather short-sighted, hadn't been aware of this attack on his person, but the Master, being much more observant, had noticed what was going on.

I think he must have been in rather a forgiving mood that day. It wasn't until I had made my direct hit, that he thought we boys had gone far enough in our bit of mischief. The raising of his finger, and a very stern look on his face, brought our bit of fun to an abrupt end, and the Rector hadn't seen a bit of it!

When we had all finished our Christmas puddings (most of us having managed a second helping), silence was called for and the Rector would address the school. He mostly commenced his speech by complimenting the Master on the excellent behaviour of all the children during the meal... After a few more words of praise, he would sometimes pass on to the subject of scrumping and other acts of mischief that we might have taken part in. He mostly ended his little talk with the hope that his orchard would give an abundance of fruit in the coming season, if for no other reason than giving his gardener a little excitement. After joining in the Lord's Prayer we were all dismissed, and on leaving school, were each given an orange. This day was always regarded as the highlight of our school year.

Stan barrowing logs at Adams Wood Farm

Stooking oats, 1932. Left: Father, Syd and
Mary, Jennie in front, with helpers

Grandfather Oliver Dowding Lane who emigrated to Australia in 1887

Father Sydney Dowding Lane, aged 21

Mother and Father in the 1926 Morris Cowley Touring Car

Rover at Adams Wood Farm

Stan, aged about nine

Boys visiting the farm as part of the
'London Boys' Country Holiday Fund,
1933. Stan, far right, Frank, third from left

An end over end
butter churn

2. Taking Stock

March 13th 1934 was a very sad day for our family. That was the day our Father died at the early age of 47. A severe cold developed into pneumonia, and he was dead within a few days. Had some of the modern drugs been available at that time, he might not have suffered such a premature death. He was buried in Stanford churchyard, and was carried there in the farm wagon, drawn by Prince, his favourite horse.

It was after his death that I learned quite a lot about his early life. He was born at Upton Court in the parish of Leysters, Herefordshire, on 12th April 1887. His mother died at his birth. She already had four children aged three to nine years.

Upton Court was an elegant Elizabethan house with quite a history attached to it. It was a mixed farm of 250 acres, and had been in the Lane family since 1705. During his occupancy of the farm, my great-grandfather built a fine set of farm buildings, all in red brick, which still look impressive to this day. Seemingly, Grandfather had fallen on bad times in the years preceding Grandmother's death. As a result he had lost most of his money and Upton Court had to be sold to pay off his creditors.

In August 1887, along with the other four children, he set off on a voyage to begin a new life in Australia. I will write more about their fate as time goes by. Father was left behind in the custody of a Mr and Mrs Cook who were old servants of my grandparents, and lived in one of the cottages at Upton Court. It was planned that, after being reared by these kindly people he would be reunited with the rest of the family in Australia. Sadly, this reunion never took place, and he never met his father or brothers. Fortunately, he had the pleasure of meeting his two sisters, Elizabeth and Edith, when they visited England in 1921.

When he became of school age he went to live with his Uncle Frank Oliver and sisters (relatives on his mother's side) at the Castle Farm, Collinton, near Leominster. He left school at the age of 12 and worked on the uncle's farm until he married my mother, Flora Gittins, in 1910. At that time his uncle set him up as tenant at the Hill Farm, Bockleton, Leominster. He remained there until moving to Adams Wood Farm in 1916. As a young boy I remember Father saying that he would go out to Australia and meet his brothers and sisters, but alas, it wasn't to be.

Mother wasn't enjoying very good health at the time of Father's death. Faced with a family of seven and a farm to deal with she had a daunting task. After several days of what must have been a very heart-breaking time, she decided to give up the farm. The older members of the family supported her in this decision and us younger ones fell in behind them - for what it was worth.

A tenant was found to take over the farm at short notice. A farm sale of all live and dead stock was arranged and took place on 21st May 1934. Quite a few tears were shed at the end of that day, as all the familiar animals and implements were taken away by their new owners.

At this period of time, farming was in the midst of a very deep depression and the prices we received for our stock were at rock bottom. From my sister-in-law 'Bea' (Arthur's widow), I have had access to the listed details of the sale. Here are some examples, all prices in LSD (pounds, shillings and pence): 12 rabbit nets £1.12s.3d; milking stools 3d; sheep dipping tank £1.9s; market trap £11; 1926 Morris Cowley Touring Car £7.10s; five Crossbred ewes & 10 lambs £20.5s; 'Tiny', a Shorthorn cow in milk £14.15s; 'Bounce' a nine-year-old Shire mare with her filly foal £46; 100-gallon cask of cider £1.10s; a Hathaway end over end butter churn £2.7s.6d; and a child's saddle and bridle £1.

My two eldest brothers, Arthur and Syd, went away to work on dairy farms where they lived as family. My two eldest sisters got posts as companion helps. In 1935 Edith became a nurse. Mary was married to Jack Dallow in the same year and provided Mother with her first grandchild, Eric, in 1936. Mother was able to rent Cheltry Cottage, close to the village of Stanford. It took some time for us younger ones - I was only 11 years old - to settle down to living in a small cottage after all the space that we had enjoyed at the farm.

I think I was the one who felt the wrench most, as I was more involved in the farm than the others. Frank by now was a boarder at Bromyard Grammar School, having passed his 11-plus and gained a scholarship. He cycled the eight miles home each weekend.

When we moved to Cheltry Cottage we took Rover with us. He was a lovely old blue and white Collie, who had been with us all his life. He was unable to settle down in his new home and, after returning to the farm several times and having to be collected, Mother asked Mr Ward, the new tenant, if he would like to keep him. That is where he stayed for the rest of his days.

The adjoining cottage to ours was occupied by the village policeman, PC Kybart. At first, when we moved in there, I thought it would be like being in prison, having to live so close to the law. After a couple of weeks we became good friends and he gave me my first-ever job. This task consisted of weeding his long garden path, and mowing his lawn each week. For this I received threepence a week. At last, I was in the money and able to stand a round of sweets at the shop in the village!

For some reason, the water from the pump in our kitchen had been condemned for drinking purposes. This handicap was the reason for my journey to the Green, a large private house about half a mile from the cottage. Mother had been given permission by the owners to use water from their well. Each morning, I used to set off with a couple of buckets, to get enough drinking water for the family's daily needs. I soon learned the amount that was needed, and made sure that my buckets were never filled to capacity. The well was 90 feet deep. Letting the heavy bucket down was easy enough, but winding it back up with the windlass was quite a heavy task. Some days at weekends, I managed to persuade brother Frank to assist in this rather dull, but very necessary task. Thankfully, before we moved from the cottage, the water was declared safe for drinking, much to my satisfaction.

Moving from one end of the parish to the other, leaving the school midway, meant that Jennie and I had to walk to school with a fresh set of companions. I did miss my donkey rides! This fresh route did have its advantages, the main one being the River Teme which we had to cross. This gave us plenty of opportunities for messing about in the water most summer afternoons. On our way home from school we would go paddling, and sometimes, if the girls were not hanging around, would discard our clothes and have an attempt at swimming. The water in the river was rarely more than a couple of feet deep, not the ideal conditions for budding Olympic swimmers, but we enjoyed it. Just over the river bridge there was an old water mill, which had been in regular use up to the turn of the century. It was built with the rather attractive red bricks which were a feature of this area. By this time it had fallen into a state of disrepair, but not bad enough to stop us spending many happy hours of play within its walls. Hide and seek was great fun, as there were lots of different compartments to get lost in. These were accessible by short, fixed ladders, most of them with a couple of rungs missing, but with all of us being young and agile, this didn't create a problem. Our biggest difficulty was getting home and having to explain why all our clothes were covered in cobwebs.

The mill is still there today and looks immaculate, after what must have been an expensive refurbishment to turn it into a very desirable private residence. Each time I pass this mill I am reminded of the dust and cobwebs that were the cause of quite a few scoldings in my younger days. Also on this route to school we passed the blacksmith's shop. He was our namesake - Jack Lane - but not a relative.

We were always welcome to stop off and spend time in the smithy, on our way home from school. I was fascinated watching the making of horseshoes out of long steel rods. After it was heated in the forge, and became red hot, the blacksmith, with the aid of a large pair of tongs, would lay the rod across the corner of his anvil and, after a few heavy strokes with his hammer, sever the right length of steel, just the correct size for one horseshoe. Then the making of the shoe would begin with the length of iron being heated until it was red hot, then hammered into the right shape. Before it was completed, with its lugs, and nail holes, it had to be put back into the forge for further heating.

The draught to the fire in the forge was created from a large set of fixed bellows. These were powered with a long handle which had to be pumped to keep the coal fire burning vigorously when needed. The blacksmith would do this operation with his one hand and, with the aid of his tongs, hold the piece of steel in the fire until hot enough to shape.

It was at this time that our presence at the forge was worthwhile, as we used to take turns at blowing the bellows, allowing the blacksmith a chance to rest his arm (that's what he told us)! It wasn't often that we were lucky enough to see any horses being shod, as they would all have been finished before our arrival. The shoes made with our help were hung up all around the smithy walls. When the horses were brought in for shoeing, the blacksmith, knowing all his customers' horses, could go to the wall and pick out just the shoes he needed for any particular horse. These would be heated again, and offered on to the horse's foot, while still hot. When the blacksmith - or farrier - was satisfied that it fitted snugly onto the foot, he would thrust the shoe into cold water to cool it down. It was then ready to be nailed on, and after a bit of rasping around the shoe, to take off any surplus hoof, that would be one foot completed.

Today, this very same smithy, that in my childhood was just the village blacksmith's, is now a thriving agricultural engineering business, servicing quite a large area of farms in the Teme Valley. It is owned, and managed, by the same family.

The village post office and sweet shop, were kept by Miss Perry, known behind her back as Black Bess. This endearing name was attributed to the fact that she was always attired in a very long black dress, reaching right down to ground level, and her crown being a head of nearly white hair. She had a temperament that suited her attire, and we kids knew exactly how to behave, when we were lucky enough to have a penny to spend on some of her sweets. One misdeed meant being told to leave the shop, and to come back the following day when, if you behaved, you would get served with your sweets.

At that time, not many households had their own telephone, but telegrams were in fairly common use. Our village post office, being only a very small one, didn't have the need for a full-time person to deliver telegrams. Miss Perry used the services of a couple of housewives from out of the village to deliver any telegrams which she received during the early part of the day. On school days, she would hold back any that arrived after midday. On these days, she would stand on the step of her shop, and await the arrival of the school children. She well knew that one or the other of them would be more than willing to deliver a telegram for her for a small reward. This reward would vary, between tuppence and sixpence, according to the distance to be travelled. Only once was I lucky enough to get a sixpenny journey, and that was to a farm on the borders of the next parish, a distance of a good couple of miles. On hearing me express doubts as to the whereabouts of this farm, one of my friends suggested that he knew the way and, for a small remuneration, he would accompany me, and put me on the right track.

Now this arrangement should have been quite sound, but for the fact that my guide took a right turn, up a very long farm track, which led us to the wrong farm, Instead, we should have gone a little further up the road, and taken a left one. After being corrected, the telegram was delivered to the right farm and each of us was rewarded with a generous slice of cake from the farmer's wife. On our long walk home, a rather heated discussion took place as to how the six pennies were to be shared out. I argued that I carried the telegram, and all he did was act as my guide, and got me lost into the bargain. Finally we decided on a 4-2 split, in my favour, but on getting the six pennies out of my pocket, my conscience must have been pricked as I handed him his two coins. Realising that I was left with twice the amount of coins, I suggested to him that we toss one of these pennies to give him a chance to equalise. He agreed readily with this idea. I tossed the coin, he called tails, and became the owner of that odd penny with his correct call.

I have often thought of the great trust that Miss Perry, the postmistress, must have placed in us children, delivering her telegrams. We always received our pay before we set off on our journey, and didn't have to report to her on completion.

During my life, the tossing of a coin has helped me make some of the major decisions that I have been faced with. When a certain problem has arisen, and after a lot of thought, and still being undecided which way to jump, I will resort to the age-old remedy and consult a coin. I have always had a ruling, that when tossing a coin, and being the sole caller, I always call heads. Heads meaning yes, and tails no, and my problem is solved! Occasionally I have cheated a little, when not being happy with the fall of the coin. Then it has to be the best of three, and that's final!

In the summer following the farm sale, and going to live in the cottage, I began to miss the activities with which I had been used to helping. Each summer during the month of June, and part of July, would be the very busy time of haymaking. The only machines we had were a mowing machine, drawn by a pair of horses, and a horse rake. In those days, the hay crops were very much lighter than those grown these days, as no chemical fertilizers were used on the meadows. The only dressing that the grass received was an occasional application of basic slag.

The turning of the hay took place a couple of days after cutting, or maybe after one if the sunshine had been extra kind. The turning was accomplished with the aid of long-handled wooden hay rakes, from which alternate teeth had been removed, to reduce their weight.

During the haymaking season we were under instructions not to waste our time on frivolous activities on our way home from school, as our presence would be required in the hay field. I can't remember any reluctance on the part of us younger members of the family to comply with this rule. On arriving at the farm we would collect a rake, and make our way to whichever meadow was ready to have its grass turned. Having arrived at the place of work we would set off in order, with the most senior member starting on the outside swath, and then each of us taking the next one and so on, keeping a safe distance apart. It was quite amazing how quickly our little team of kids could turn a few acres of hay. I never looked on the job as a bore, quite the opposite; I used to love it, as did my brothers and sisters.

One of the highlights of these lovely summer days spent in the hayfields were the picnics that always followed the completion of the afternoon session. Mother, along with one of my elder sisters, would arrive carrying baskets of bread and jam, buttered lardy cakes, and great slices of fruit cake, which were always cleared up, right down to the last crumb, with quite a bit of help from myself.

In the year before Father's death he purchased a second-hand, horse-drawn, Albion swath turner. Although this spelt the end of our importance in the hay field, it did mean that we were able to pursue our other activities. The following year this machine was sold in the farm sale, along with all the other equipment.

About 20 acres of cereals were grown each year, wheat, oats and sometimes a couple of acres of beans. We had a McCormick self binder which was used to reap our own corn, and Father always used to reap the crops at Broomy Fields Farm, our immediate neighbour. Mr Postins, the owner, used to lend us one of his horses to make up a team of three to pull this binder. The sheaves were put into stooks of six and I can remember, on some occasions, being allowed to help stook them. This was a job that had to done just right, as these stooks had to stand for a week or so and, in the case of oats, much longer. There was an old saying that "oats should hear the church bells ring on three successive Sundays", before they were ready to cart and stack.

On the days when reaping would be going on at home, great haste would be made back from school. The reason for this being the fact that we wanted to be in on the final act of rabbit running. Much excitement would take place as the patch of corn gradually got smaller and, at this stage, the rabbits would run out of the corn, and make a dash back to their holes, which were mostly in the surrounding hedgerows. It was on this journey that we tried to intercept them, sometimes with success, but quite often some of them escaped and survived to live another day! I look back on these exciting days and still think that the ones that got away gave the most fun, as these rewarded us with a much better chase than the unfortunate ones that got caught. Mother used to make some delicious rabbit pies out of our catch. I am sure the fact that I had helped to catch the contents of those pies made them so much more tasty!

After spending its given time in the stooks, the corn was carted and stacked into the French barn to await the arrival of the threshing machine later in the year.

The threshing of the small amount of corn which was grown on our farm would take a couple of days. At this time some of the neighbours joined forces, to create a big-enough gang to make the job go smoothly. Now, threshing days were the cause of a bit of deceit on my part. My two elder brothers, having obtained permission to have the day off school to help, weren't too sympathetic to my pleas to stay with them. They told me that *they* had had to wait to be considered old enough to help in such a manly job, and that the day would come when I would be old enough to enjoy the same privilege. I recollect the devious excuses that I thought up to enable me to be kept home from school for that day.

One such day a very bad tummy ache was a good enough reason why it wouldn't be safe for me to attend class. But as the morning progressed, I was seen running round the barn with a big stick, chasing the poor little mice as they emerged from out of the corn. It was noticed that the pains must have disappeared very quickly; for this untruth, I quite rightly got a severe reprimand.

On another day, I suddenly developed a sore throat, just as we were getting ready for school. I was given the benefit of the doubt and allowed to be excused. That day proved to be rather a disastrous one for me. By about 9.30am, with Frank and Jennie safely off to school, my throat suddenly took a turn for the better. After a bit of pleading that I would feel so much better out in the fresh air, I was allowed out. After an hour or so watching all the activities around the threshing machine, I ventured around the back of the barn to see if the mice had started to escape from the corn. About once each month the Rev. Hewit was in the habit of calling to visit my parents, mostly in the afternoon, and would stay and enjoy a cup of tea with them. On this day, much to my dismay, he made a morning visit. Just as I arrived at the back of the barn I spotted him, dressed in his plus-four tweed suit and deer stalker hat, strolling along carrying a large, gnarled thumb stick. As he spotted me he called out, "Stanley why aren't you at school this morning?"

"Sir, I have got a sore throat," was my answer.

"Then what are you doing out here in the cold, with that big stick you are waving about?" came his reply.

After telling him I was about to start chasing the mice as they came out of the stack, he asked, "For what reason are you doing such a thing?"

"Well Sir, I am trying to kill them, as they are a big pest around the farm." Instead of getting a good telling-off from him, for such a feeble excuse, he just said, "Good lad, make sure you don't let any of them get away!" How wrong can one be!

During the year we spent at Cheltry Cottage, feeling very much lost without our own farm, I was delighted one day when Mother told me that she had received a letter from my Uncle Will (her eldest brother) inviting me to spend the whole of my holiday with them. September was the month that we always had off, and it was known as the hop picking holiday. During this month the Teme Valley, which was the main hop growing area of Worcestershire, was inundated with a vast number of families arriving for the hopping. All the hop farms had a number of huts in which these families would live. Most of these folk came from Dudley, Tipton, Walsall, and other towns in the black country. We country boys (and girls) had quite a difficulty in understanding their dialect, nevertheless we all managed to get along well together, and picked up some of their town habits, and a few more words to add to our limited vocabulary. That year, however, I was quite happy to forego all the excitement of the hop yards, as I was sure that my holiday spent on my uncle's farm would be more to my liking. The Ford Farm at Middleton-On-The-Hill, had been in the Gittins family since 1871. My mother was born there, as were her twelve brothers and sisters. Grandfather Gittins farmed it up until his retirement in 1916. At this time Uncle Will took over the farm, having vacated Adams Wood Farm, enabling Father to take over that tenancy.

The Ford Farm was a typical mixed farm of 190 acres, which supported a suckler herd of Hereford cattle, and a flock of Clun forest sheep. During the month that I stayed there I helped my cousin to prepare some rams from this flock to go to the sales. The prices obtained for these rather smartly clipped rams ranged from £5 to £8 apiece.

Also at this time, a bunch of Hereford steers were being fed a large sack of nuts each day. These were dispersed from the back of the trap that my uncle drove around the farm every morning. Each Tuesday of that holiday I, along with Jim, a boy who worked on the farm, was detailed to drive a couple of steers to Tenbury Wells weekly market.

This was a journey of about five miles along a quiet road. The steers were grossly over-fat by today's standards, very docile, and much better behaved than some others I have had to deal with over the years. The weight of these cattle ranged from 15 to 17 hundredweight(cwts) apiece, and they were sold by auction, for about 23 to 25 shillings per live cwt.

After the market was over, we got taken back to the farm by car, except on one occasion. This day there was a sale of breeding sheep after the sale of the cattle. Standing round the ring with my cousin, watching the various pens of ewes being sold by auction, for between 18 and 32 shillings apiece, I was pleased when the auctioneer knocked down a pen of 25 young ewes to him for 29 shillings apiece.

On being asked if we felt fit to drive these sheep out to the farm, both Jim and I assured my cousin that we were. After being treated to a good dinner, in the market cafe, we set off with our little flock. We were progressing along the road at just a good pace when, about a mile into our journey, an old Model T Ford car passed us, and pulled up in front on the grass verge. Out jumped three men, and the one who must have been the boss, said, "These are not your sheep," and promptly started to drive them back in the direction from which they came. This was rather a serious situation for two boys to be faced with, no sheep and not knowing what to do. Jim at the age of 16 was five years my senior and, after a short period of bewilderment, decided that we should carry on with our journey back to the farm, and explain the absence of our flock. Just a short while before this bit of rustling took place, my uncle and cousin had overtaken us in their car, and as they were passing, had called out a word of praise on how well we had got our little flock under control. Arriving back at the farm, minus our sheep, it didn't take long to convince them what had gone wrong. They made a quick journey back into the market to get an explanation from the auctioneer, as to the reason for this incident. Seemingly, the vendor had placed a reserve price of 30 shillings apiece on these ewes, and on hearing that the auctioneer had sold them for 29 shillings, wasn't at all pleased and wasn't willing for the deal to go through. Having found which direction they were heading, he set off in his old battered car to rescue his sheep.

The outcome of this exercise meant that three parties lost out that day; the vendor didn't have a sale, the auctioneer didn't get his commission, and my cousin didn't get his bargain.

I had only met my Grandfather and Grandmother Gittins a few times and those were very brief encounters. They came to visit us at Adams Wood once in awhile, but I looked on those meetings more with awe than pleasure. They would arrive by their pony and trap and, after alighting, one of my elder brothers would stable the pony. Father and Mother would entertain them in the sitting room, with all us children waiting in the kitchen. In order of age we went in, two at a time, just for a few minutes. I can't remember anything of these visits, except for very severe bouts of shyness. I am sure my Grandparents (both of whom lived into their mid 80s), were just as ill at ease with us, as we were with them. They had 39 grandchildren, and that's a lot of kids to put names and faces to, when seen only once in a while.

On this particular day, my uncle who was going into Leominster on some business, suggested that he would drop me off at Grandmother's, and collect me on his return. She was now a widow and had been living in Leominster for a few years. My knock on the door was answered by Miss Pound who was Grandmother's nursemaid.

After explaining to her who I was, she invited me into the hall, and asked me to follow her into the sitting room, where Grandmother, now in her 86th year, was dozing in her chair. On hearing that one of her grandsons had come to pay her a visit, she asked, "And which one may that be?" On being informed that it was Stanley, she pondered for a while, and said, "Ah, Stanley! Stanley! Ah, that's Flora's youngest isn't he? That's the naughty one!"

With this rather disappointing introduction, I was a little bit lost for words, and after sitting in silence for what I thought was ages, and with Grandmother dozing off again, I was wishing I had stayed back helping on the farm. Wondering how I could relieve my boredom, I asked the nursemaid if I might have an apple. I was told that I could go out into the garden, pick one off the tree and stay out there to eat it. Not only did I eat one, but also stuffed my pockets with more of those delicious Worcester Permains. With me being the third youngest of her 39 grandchildren, calling on her unexpectedly in the middle of her afternoon snooze probably wasn't the best of ideas.

I look back with sadness on that one and only time that I saw Grandmother alone. She died the following year in 1935.

I never did see my paternal grandparents. One day when I was about six years of age, a telegram arrived at Adams Wood, with the sad news that Grandfather Lane had died at his farm near Townsville in Queensland, Australia. He had gone out there with his four eldest children in 1887, with what little money he had left, after settling with his creditors on the sale of Upton Court.

I sincerely hope that our grandchildren will have shared a much closer bond with us, than ever I was blessed with my own grandparents.

After getting home from this holiday at my uncle's, and having been so pleased to get back into life on the farm, I then decided that one day I was going to have my own farm. This wasn't to be for a good many years, but the ambition remained until it was achieved all that time later.

In the summer of 1935 Mother, having received the final settlement from the sale of live and dead stock from Adams Wood, decided that she had enough money to go ahead and buy her own house, instead of staying in the rented cottage. The four elder members of the family were all settled in good jobs, and living at their place of work. The farm had been let to a good tenant and was providing her with an income, just about sufficient for the rest of us.

Country houses in those days didn't come onto the market as often as they do at the present time. After looking over several properties in our own locality, and being unable to find one that was satisfactory, Mother started to look further afield. Eventually, she found a nice house in the village of Abbeydore, which is situated in the beautiful Golden Valley at the foothills of the Black Mountains in Herefordshire.

Moving to this new home, 35 miles away from Stanford, was a great milestone in my life. Leaving Adams Wood for Cheltry Cottage had been a wrench, but this move in the autumn of 1935 meant that Jennie (my youngest sister) and I would have to leave Stanford School and start afresh at a new one, leaving all our friends behind.

On the afternoon of the last day that we attended school, Mr Williams, the master, addressed the class, and told them how sad it was for the last members of the Lane family to be leaving. A few tears came to my eyes when he referred to us as a well-behaved and trusted family, and hoped that Jennie and I would be happy in our new school.

Upton Court, Leysters, Herefordshire, the birthplace of Stan's father

Stan, standing, and Frank, on a
borrowed horse, 1933

Stan, left, and Frank,
Cheltry Cottage 1934

3. The Budding Farmer

Bryn-Y-Nant was the name of our new house in Abbeydore. It was a big improvement on the cottage we had been living in at Stanford, as it boasted a bathroom with hot and cold running water, a flush toilet and two bay windows. It stood in its own fair-sized patch of ground, on a slight slope facing the village. It also had a good-sized garage, which conveniently housed Mother's recently acquired, secondhand Austin 7 car. The care of the garden and lawn became my task, with a little help from brother Frank, when he wasn't too heavily engaged with homework. He had been transferred to Hereford Grammar School. His daily journey to school involved a three-mile bike ride to Pontrilas, where he caught a train into Hereford, a further 12 miles.

Jennie and I had just 150 yards to walk to the village school. In the early days of life in our new home, this luxurious way of getting to school soon gave way to nostalgia on my part. I missed the long walk, and the companionship of the other children on the morning and afternoon journeys, plus the fact that not many side attractions were available on this short route! The village consisted of the Church of England school and school house, situated on a triangle at the end of the short street, three farms and four cottages. The Mill Farm doubled up as the post office and shop, and Mr Watkins, the owner, milked a few cows, and delivered their milk with a pony and trap in and around the village. Milk bottles were not in use at this time in the very rural areas, instead the milk would be carried in two gallon buckets, each with a shiny brass handled lid. Inside the bucket would hang a pint measure and also a half-pint one, which were used to ladle into the housekeeper's jug the quantity he required that day. This method of milk distribution was still in use in some areas until the 1950s.

The Dore Abbey and Rectory were just on the edge of the village, with the local pub, The Neville Arms, close by. The name of Abbeydore is derived from the Cistercian Abbey that was built in the 12th century, and the River Dore which flows through the middle of the parish. This river rises near Dorstone up in the Black Mountains, and flows the full length of the Golden Valley, joining the River Monnow near Pontrilas.

The Golden Valley is so named because of its wonderful display of wild daffodils that are such a sight in the meadows each spring. The one pasture that was particularly impressive was the parkland at Bacton

Court. This park of some 70 acres lies on a slight hillside, is studded with trees, and really is a sight to be seen. Sadly, some of these pastures had to be ploughed up during World War Two, to help provide extra food for our country. Now, 60 years later, those daffodils have never returned in the profusion that I remember as a boy.

The Golden Valley Railway ran from Hay-on-Wye down through the valley, and connected with the main South Wales line at Pontrilas. It had been built at the turn of the century, mainly to serve the farming community that lived in the valley. I don't think it could have been much of a money spinner for Great Western Railways, but it was very popular as a means of transport. There was just one daily train each way, with an extra one on the weekly market day at Hereford. There were five stations, each served by a station master, who led a very leisurely life. On his day off, the train driver, who was the sole member of the crew, would stop at each level crossing, get off the train, open the gates, then remount and drive the train alongside the platform. With the aid of a duplicate key, he opened the door to the station master's office and issued tickets to the very few passengers who were waiting.

After loading whatever goods were for dispatch into the goods wagon, he had the task of closing the level-crossing gates once more. As our house was close to the station, and if I happened to be at home and heard the train approaching, I would race to the crossing and open the gates for him. One evening, each May, a special train was run for the benefit of anyone wishing to spend an evening visiting the May Fair at Hay-on-Wye.

I well remember the one and only time that I visited this Fair. Mother gave me a half crown to go and enjoy myself with the other boys. This was a very generous sum of money in those days, and it should have ensured me plenty of fun on the various side shows. After spending sixpence on my return rail fair, I was left with a florin, which I handed to the attendant on the dodgem cars, the ride we boys had chosen (at two pence a time) as the start to our evening entertainment. This man told me he would bring me the change at the end of the ride. Alas, this promise wasn't kept and on me reminding him of this misdeed, I was told that he had already given me my change. This is the only time in my life that I have knowingly been cheated of money. It was quite a depressing experience, to be left penniless and the evening's fun at the Fair just begun. The two other boys came to my rescue and shared their pocket money with me. After this affair, I always made sure that I only gave the correct money on any fair rides.

41

The train journey home that night was quite an exciting one. The driver told us, as we entered the single carriage, that he would be quite happy to drop any of us off at any point between stations, if it meant a shorter walk home. This suggestion met with ready approval from several of the passengers, and they soon explained to him where they would like him to stop. This operation went well, except for one slight error on the part of the driver. He had been requested to stop two miles out of Dorstone Station, but failed to keep his promise. The three young people who were expecting to alight at this point found themselves still chugging along, but not to be outdone, they wound down the window and started to wave one of their outer garments, with the hope of catching the driver's eye. About a mile further along the track towards Peterchurch he caught sight of their frantic waving and brought the train to a halt. Realising what was wrong, he started to steam back along the line to the point where he had promised to stop. The driver and the three grateful passengers met out on the line, and the driver was heard to say how sorry he was, to have caused them a few anxious moments, thinking that they would have a much longer walk home from the next station. I doubt if British Rail would look kindly on this kind of service in the modern age. Sadly, the Golden Valley Line was closed in 1946.

Just across the road from Bryn-Y-Nant was the entrance to Upper House Farm. Here lived five members of the Lloyd family, all of them engaged in the running of their 400-acre farm. I soon made friends with all of them, and got involved in most of the activities that they carried out. Longing to get into farm life again, this was a godsend to me, and I exploited it to the full. Apart from helping Mother with a few odd jobs, and attending to the garden, I spent all my time over at the farm, helping with any job that was on the go.

Everything on this farm revolved around the wellbeing of the Shire horses, who appeared to me to be the most important animals of all. They numbered 37 at the time I was privileged to help with them. Six of them were brood mares, who along with three young geldings, were the workhorse force for the farm. The geldings, along with a couple of young mares, were under the sole care of John, the eldest of the Lloyd brothers. The rest were of various ages from one to four years.

These young horses were broken in at three years of age and were mostly sold as five-year-olds. At this age they were sold at the special Shire horse sales at Hereford. In the year 1936 I had the pleasure of going to the sale where Captain, the Lloyds' horse, was being offered for sale. Saturday was the day of the sale, so it didn't mean me taking a day off school (not that it would have deterred me anyway). At that time, Shire-horse breeding was a very important part of the farming scene in those border counties. Hereford, Craven Arms and Newtown were the three main centres for the sales. Quite a number of these horses would be bought by farmers from far afield, with several of them going to work in the hop gardens of Kent.

The very elite would be bought by the brewers or the railways to work as dray horses in the cities. On this particular day there were 80 horses for sale, and I must say the sight of them, with their tails and manes dressed up with bright ribbons, is something to remember. When Captain came into the ring he looked superb, and the auctioneer described him as the best five-year-old in the sale. 75 guineas was the top price of the day, and it was Captain who achieved it, much to our delight. He was bought for Ansells brewery and joined their stables in Birmingham, where he probably spent the rest of his life as a dray horse, delivering barrels of ale to the city's pubs.

The brood mares mostly foaled in April, but by hay time in June, they had to join the workforce. Each morning, these mares with their foals were brought from the paddock into the yard, caught and harnessed, leaving the foals secure in the yard. At lunchtimes, wherever on the farm these mares happened to be working, they had to be unhitched, brought back to the farm and loosed into the yard to allow the foals to suckle. This operation was repeated again at teatime if the men were working late, which they often were. A few hours each day were spent on this exercise, as things didn't always go as they should. Some of the mares became restless after being parted from their offspring for any length of time and, with half a chance, would make for home, a situation that demanded skilful restraint on the part of the waggoners.

There were three magnificent stallions at the head of the stud. During the breeding season, these stallions, each of them handled by a groom, travelled the whole of the Golden Valley, and some of the surrounding hills. The grooms had been engaged in this work for years, and they were familiar with all the farms that had any brood mares, and also knew when they were likely to be in season. I seem to remember being told by Tom Lawrence, the senior of these grooms, that for each mare that was served by their stallion, they were entitled to a groom's fee of half a crown, and if she conceived and gave birth to a foal, he got paid a further five shillings. For this final payment, he would have to wait 'til the following season, which was quite an incentive in those days. These men would find accommodation for themselves and the stallion at various farms on the route, only returning to the home farm on Saturdays. Early each Monday morning they set off on their rounds again, the stallions immaculately turned out, each of them with a pack saddle containing the groom's equipment and a certain amount of corn for the horse. These grooms took a great deal of pride in their personal appearance and would arrive back at the farm on a Saturday, looking just as smart as they did when they set out on the Monday. In the winter of 1936 one stallion, Rob-Roy, was taken by rail up to a Shire horse show in Islington in London. To the great disappointment of John Lloyd, he only managed a second place in his class.

The farm ran a flock of Welsh Mountain sheep, and a suckler herd of Hereford cattle. The sheep were mostly confined to the hill pastures, whilst the cattle grazed the very lush pastures adjoining the River Dore. During the winter the cows were all tied up in a long shed containing 30 stalls and, twice a day, were let out into the yard, where they drank from the stream that ran the full length of the farmyard. This stream was of very clear water and had a hard bottom to it, and was the only source of drinking water for all the livestock adjacent to it. Being an autumn calving herd, the calves were all housed in a large pen at the end of the cowshed. Twice a day they were let out to join their mothers and, after suckling them, were rather reluctant to be returned to their pen.

My first experience of milking was with the flock of Welsh ewes. About four days after their lambs had been weaned, and sold at the Hay-on-Wye sheep sales, they were all rounded up and penned, ready to be milked out - purely as a precaution against mastitis. Seeing the three men get started on the job prompted me to have a go, and I was soon shown how to get stuck in. The ewe was turned up and sat on her haunch, making sure she didn't sit on her tail. The milking was done by directing the milk through the hind legs onto the ground. The udders were full of milk and the ewes must have been relieved to be rid of it. After rather a slow start, I soon got the hang of it, and by the end of the day was feeling rather pleased with myself, having been allowed to help milk out the flock of 400 sheep. I believe this operation was carried out after another period of four days, but that being a school day I wasn't able to assist with it, much to my annoyance, as it would have been more to my liking than a day of boring lessons.

After my day of helping with milking the sheep I thought it was about time that I should be learning to milk cows, as by now, I was determined that I would be getting a job on a dairy farm when I left school, in the not-too-distant future. There were two house cows on the farm, both of them very quiet animals. For a couple of weeks, I was allowed to milk the one whilst Bert Lloyd milked the other. In this time I had got quite good at the job and suggested to Bert that I would like to be allowed to milk both of them. With him having plenty of other jobs to be getting on with, he was only to pleased to hand over to me, as long as I milked them night and morning without fail, each day except Sundays.

Mrs Lloyd, on hearing of this arrangement, said no way was I going to be allowed to do this job just for the love of it, and I was to be paid half a crown a week. That is the sum I collected every Friday evening until I left school. Without fail, on receiving my wage each week, I went down to the Post Office and bought five sixpenny National saving stamps. 20 of these stamps would buy a National Savings certificate worth 10 shillings. In the period of this (lucrative) job I saved all of them, not cashing any until my marriage in 1948, by which time they had become worth 17s,6d each, which wasn't a fortune, but it gave me a good deal of satisfaction to have hung onto them since my early teenage years. The milking of these cows each morning didn't interfere with school times, as being so close to home, I used to be finished by eight o'clock, home to breakfast, and after a three-minute walk be at school.

By now, anyone reading these few notes will probably have gathered the impression that school wasn't my main source of pleasure in those early days. Quite right, it wasn't. Now, at 82 years of age, I regret not paying more attention to the little education that was available to me at the two village schools that I attended. At Stanford I got along quite well, and kept up with the other children; very rarely would I have been considered the 'Weakest Link'.

My arrival at Abbeydore School caused the Headmistress, Mrs Thickens, a certain amount of frustration. She, along with the aged Infant teacher, had this cosy little village school all to themselves, with only 28 children, aged five to 14 to teach. To have another 12-year-old boy thrust upon her was just about as much as she could cope with. Having to rearrange one of the desks, find an extra seat and sort out a few books and a pencil was more than she could bear. Once she got me seated, she told me that the other children in the class would soon put me right on the lessons that we were taking. My sister Jennie, being two years my junior, fitted more cosily into her little world and was made very welcome in the class. I soon made friends with my new classmates, much to the annoyance of the Head.

Each morning, we all joined in the singing of a hymn after saying morning prayers. The Rector used to attend this gathering at least twice a week. It was at this assembly that the Head brought him up-to-date with any misbehaviour on the part of the children. I someway think that there was little love lost between these two leaders of the school. An incident that reminds me of this lack of harmony took place after the Golden Valley Annual Ploughing Match in October 1936. This was to be held at a farm at Vowchurch, a distance of four miles from the school.

The Lloyds had entered one three-horse plough team and several other Shire horses into the show that accompanied the match. I had been asked if I would like to lead one of the three-year-old geldings to this event, to which I proudly consented. Unfortunately, this show was to take place on a Wednesday and would cause a slight problem. Along with two other boys, who also had family interests in the show, we politely asked the Head if we could have a day off school to attend.

"Certainly not," came her definite reply.

The situation called for further discussion among the remainder of the boys, and the overwhelming decision was that we would all take part in this day off and go to the match. As it turned out, when the day came, a few of the girls added their support and came to the show. We had a most enjoyable day, only to be met (quite rightly) with the wrath of the Head on the following morning. She would be informing the Rector on his next visit about the gross misconduct of the class. On the Friday morning following this event the Rector turned up and led the class in morning prayer. At the conclusion of the hymn singing, the teacher informed him of the misdeeds that our class had indulged in. Without hesitation he replied, "Well now, I expect they have learned far more than at any day at school!"

I have seen many looks of anger on people's faces at different times but never one of the intensity of hers. As red-as-a-beetroot she faced the class that morning.

Most mornings, four boys were detailed to follow the horse teams that had gone out to work earlier on, collect any droppings and bring them back for use in the school garden. Armed with a bucket and coal shovel, we would set off in whichever direction the horses had travelled that morning.

This delegation of jobs was of the utmost importance to the boys, as it enabled us to miss at least half a morning lesson. We always walked to the gate where the teams had left the road to enter the fields, and then started our collection on the homeward run. Sometimes our buckets would be full before we got back to the school garden and emptied them, which meant another journey to complete the job. Occasionally we cheated, and shovelled the last few droppings out of sight under the hedge, as we might have been considered not up to our job, had it been reported that horse muck had been sighted on the road after our morning task of collecting it. I wonder what classification this kind of schoolwork would fit into in today's National Curriculum. Looking back I don't think it did much to aid my academic learning! Having collected this valuable commodity, it then became our job to spread it around the vegetable patch, and dig it in. The ensuing crops from this garden then called for our help once again when they were ready for picking. This task was usually carried out by just two of us. We took it in turns to pick and shell peas (delicious!), dig and skin potatoes, pull and scrape carrots, and whatever else needed picking. Raspberries and strawberries were both absent from that garden. Do you have any idea why?

One morning the organ tuner called to ask the teacher if one of her boys could assist him for most of the day. He had been asked to tune the organ in the Abbey and needed someone to do the blowing for him.

"Stanley, would you like to go and assist this gentleman for the day?" was the teacher's response. I quickly agreed to this request, thinking to myself what an unexpected stroke of good luck to miss school. I am sure she also felt a sense of good fortune to be shot of me for the day. At the end of the day's organ blowing, I was given half a crown by the tuner, which made the day doubly rewarding for me.

My parents had been great card players, and encouraged the whole family to partake in it. During the winter evenings, long before the days of television, it was up to everyone to create their own entertainment, and card playing was a very popular way of keeping occupied for hours on end. At the age of 12, just after going to live at Abbeydore, I succeeded in persuading Mother to let me start going to whist drives. These were held at Bacton Village Hall, a distance of two miles from home. This parish didn't have its own school, and the few children who lived there attended our school at Abbeydore. Two of these children who were regular supporters of these whist drives were the main cause of my constant requests to be allowed join them each Friday evening.

My first attendance at one of these drives was a little bit awe-inspiring, as most of the whist players were adults and quite a few of them were ladies in their more advanced years, and were on the lookout for bad play of any kind. I got through the 24 hands with only one severe reprimand from my partner, and that only came as a result of me playing a wrong card, and causing the loss of one trick. The second time that I went I steered clear of this certain lady, but alas, in the game of progressive whist you can't avoid any player for too long, and in this case, I soon found myself at a table acting as her partner. After the previous week's telling off I was a little on the nervous side, dreading that I might make an even bigger blunder this evening, but all went well and we won the hand by two tricks. She even praised the way that I had played my cards. After this piece of encouragement I looked on her in a more kindly light.

Rabbits were quite a problem in that part of the country, and the Lloyds' farm seemed to have more than its fair share of them. During the winter months Bert used to spend a considerable amount of time ferreting and netting them, and worked the whole way round the farm during the season. I showed enough interest in this exercise to be asked to help with it, and I soon found myself hurrying home from school on these days. A Welsh Mountain pony was kept at the farm, and I used to catch and bridle him, and ride bareback to whatever part of the farm I knew the ferreting was taking place. Most of the days I was able to assist with the end of the ferreting before darkness fell. I was quite happy to remove the rabbits from the nets, and kill them with a sharp blow on the back of the head. But when it came to catching the ferrets I must admit that I was a bit of a coward and only did it under extreme verbal encouragement from the handler. My caution in picking them up was a result of helping to rid a stack of wheat that was infested with rats. Bert told me to stand at the far end of the stack and watch out for the ferret in case he came out at my end. After waiting for what seemed ages, he appeared at one of the rat holes about five feet off the ground. I thought, now was the chance to show my worth, and went to catch this small animal, but he beat me to it and caught me first! He nabbed me between my thumb and finger, and had no intentions of letting go, so in my shame I crept round to the other side of the stack and was relieved of my burden by a very amused Bert! As a result of this little mishap, I have treated ferrets with great respect ever since and given them as wide a berth as possible.

The day's catch of rabbits varied between 30 and 50 and, on one exceptional day, the bag was over 70. The rabbits were threaded onto a couple of ropes and then slung over the pony's back and carried back to the farm, where they were paunched and made ready to be taken to the station the following morning. They would arrive at Birmingham market before midday and be on sale less than 24 hours after being caught. The price that the Lloyds received for them was between 10 pence and a shilling each. In those lean, pre-war days of the 1930s, although the rabbits were classed as pests, they were also a source of extra revenue. The price received for 35 rabbits would pay one farm worker's wages for a six-day week. What would the ratio be today?

Another job I did in the summer of 1936 was to catch this same pony and collect from the farmhouse two stone jars, each containing a gallon of cider, sling them across his back and take them up to the hayfields. Most of these fields lay on the valley bottom, adjacent to the railway line. With there being no trains travelling the line in the middle of the afternoon, it was considered quite safe to make use of it.

I was instructed to take the track as it was a much quicker route than going through the fields, which would entail the opening and closing of a number of gates. The pony, having no shoes, and not caring too much for treading on the course gravel that lay on the track, soon got the knack of walking on the wooden sleepers only. The men working in the hayfield were always pleased to see me and the pony plodding along, getting ever nearer with a very welcome drop of their favourite brew. After handing the jars over the wire to one of the men I would ride off back to the farm. One day I became quite alarmed, as in the distance I could see a small carriage approaching at a fair pace. I became a little worried, thinking that I was in dead trouble for trespassing on the railway line.

As this object drew nearer, I recognised it as one of those hand-operated tenders that were used on the railways for the transport of men and their tools to carry out maintenance work on the line. I dismounted and led the pony as far down the embankment as possible, thinking that they might pass by and ignore me. Not them, the one with the peaked cap (must have been the boss), asked me why I was on the track with a pony. When I explained to him that I had been making a delivery of cider to some very thirsty haymakers, he smiled, and said he only wished he had met me before I had handed it over to them, as he was sure they wouldn't have missed a couple of swigs!

That same year marked another milestone in my life. I was allowed to do some horse-raking. After the main crop had been raked and carted, the whole area had to be raked again, not a strand was allowed to be wasted. On the farm there was a half-legged horse (a Shire crossed with any smaller breed) by the name of Plym, who was very quiet to work and walked at quite a good pace. It was decided that I was capable of undertaking this task and John, the senior of the brothers, told me how to go about it. First, I had to harness the horse correctly, and then hitch him up to the horse-rake and adjust the driving reins, so that they were just the right length to enable me to sit on the seat without any left to dangle. I was to rake every bit of the fields and tip the rake at intervals of about 100 yards, and make sure that each of the rows was kept straight.

I think they were satisfied with my work, and I was awarded a 10-shilling note at the end of the season. Considering that I had horse-raked about 120 acres over a period of several weeks, I don't think I was overpaid, but I felt so pleased with myself having being allowed to do such a worthwhile job.

The two classrooms in Abbeydore School were each heated by a cylindrical, enclosed stove, and it was the job of the four eldest boys to take turns and service these stoves each morning. This involved raking out the spent ash, and filling up the scuttles with a supply of coke, enough for the day's needs. This job-sharing arrangement had worked smoothly for the first year that I attended the school, but in the winter of 1936 the teacher, for some reason unknown to me, told me that I was to do this job each day on my own. Not being afraid of work I just got on with it, but the other three boys thought that I was being unfairly treated. After a week or so of gentle persuasion from my three friends, I decided to make a protest about my daily chore.

After prayers on this particular morning, the teacher said, "Stanley, will you go and attend to the stoves?"

"No Ma'am," was my reply, said in a very subdued voice.

"Why ever not?" she demanded.

"Well Ma'am, I don't think it quite fair, that I should have to do this job every morning, whilst the other boys are quite willing to take their share of it."

She replied, "I am the person who says who does what in my classroom, and I am asking you again, Stanley, will you attend to the stoves?"

"No Ma'am!" was my reply for the second time.

By now her face was turning quite red, and I was beginning to shake in my shoes, but was determined to carry on with my protest. After my fourth refusal to her request, she had the last say, and asked (or rather told) me to leave the classroom and go home. On my arrival at home, Mother was very cross, not so much with me but with the teacher, who she thought had been wrong in the manner that she unfairly set out the daily jobs. I am not proud of this episode that happened all those years ago, but can honestly say that was the only act of militancy I have ever been involved in.

During my time at Abbeydore School there was another small

episode that rather upset me. One day the Head received a booklet from the Cadbury Chocolate Company inviting the class to write an essay on the growing and harvesting of the cocoa bean, the main ingredient of chocolate. A leaflet was passed around the class explaining the whole operation, and the following day we were given one full lesson to write this essay. At the conclusion of this work each of us wrote our name at the head of it and handed it to the teacher.

About two weeks later the postman delivered rather an impressive-looking parcel to the school. The class was inquisitive to know what was in it, as it was a rare occasion for anything like this to arrive. At the end of the lesson our minds were set at rest as the Head announced that it was a parcel of chocolate from Cadbury's. On opening it, a colourful card presented itself and Mrs Thickens, after adjusting her spectacles and getting rather red in the face, announced: "Stanley Lane is the winner of the Cadbury Essay and here is his prize", which she handed to me without any sign of congratulations whatsoever. The class did indulge in some rather boisterous hand-clapping, much to the teacher's displeasure. The parcel contained eight four-ounce bars of different flavoured chocolate, some of which I shared with my classmates.

Stan's mother, Flora, at Bryn-Y-Nant

Stan with Shire foal at seven to eight weeks old

4. The Cow That Jumped Over The Shed

I never went back to Abbeydore School after the stove affair, but spent the last term of my school life at Ewyas Harold School which was a distance of three miles away at the bottom of the Golden Valley. Knowing that this was my final term before going out to start work, I don't recollect anything of any consequence that took place in that period, other than I was eagerly waiting for the last day of term to arrive, and allow me to get started in my first fulltime job.

My eldest brother Arthur had discussed with Mother the idea of me going to work on the same farm where he was employed. This was at the Valley Farm at Fockbury in Worcestershire, where he had been working since Father's death in 1934. Mother wasn't enjoying the best of health at this time and had decided to move back to the Worcester area to be closer to my two elder sisters. At last the day I had been waiting for had arrived and, now aged 14, on the morning of Good Friday 1937 Mother drove me over to the Valley Farm, and I helped with the milking that same afternoon.

I spent four and a half very happy years working there, with Arthur keeping a fatherly eye on me and making sure that I kept on my best behaviour, whilst living in the farmhouse with Mr and Mrs Evans, our bosses.

The Valley was a tenanted farm of 90 acres, with extra land being hired for the making of hay, and grazing of dry cows. At that time the area around Fockbury was witnessing an increase in its population, due to the growth in production of Austin cars at their Longbridge factory. This situation was exploited by several dairy farmers in that area, Reg Evans being one of these. With the help of Arthur, he had built up a considerable retail milk round, selling all the milk produced at the Valley, and often having to buy in from a couple of the neighbouring farmers.

This operation wasn't strictly legal, as since the formation of the Milk Marketing Board (MMB) in 1933, they became the sole buyers of all milk produced. The only exception to this order were the farmers with 'producer retailer licences', and farmhouse cheese and butter makers. Each month, these producers had to pay a small levy to the MMB. This ruling wasn't very popular, as it meant keeping records of all the gallons of milk produced on the farm, and sending the returns complete with cheque by a given day each month. Form filling was no more of a popular sport among farmers than is the case today.

When I started work at the Valley the dairy herd consisted mostly of about 25 Shorthorn cows, which grew to 50 in the years that I spent there. It was a 'flying herd' and had quite a high turnover of cows. To keep up a constant supply of milk meant having plenty of fresh calvers in the herd and this was achieved by buying them in from the weekly sales of dairy cattle at Bromsgrove or Kidderminster markets. To make space for these new entrants, some of the low yielders were sold as culls, mostly for a reasonable price.

Reg Evans always bought the best cows on offer, and on my asking him what he had paid for them, he always replied with his favourite stock phrase, "Money and fair words!" and would then give me a proper answer. The costs ranged from £18 up to £24, but at the outbreak of war in 1939, they had crept up to around £28 apiece. One day in Kidderminster market he must have had a lapse in his good judgement and bought rather a shifty-looking Cocked Horned cow for £12. During the afternoon's milking on the day of her arrival at the farm, Bill Rutter, the cowman, sat down to milk her. Now Bill, who was a very placid, easy-going chap, was abruptly reminded that life wasn't always quite so peaceful. This cow started to get fidgety as soon as he started to milk her, and by the time he had got a dozen or so squeezes out of her it became obvious that no great friendship had developed between them.

Very rarely was Bill heard to utter any swear words, but Arthur and I, who happened to be milking further down the shed, were amazed to hear that he could use so many of them at such short notice, in telling this cow about her uncertain parentage. Whether she didn't believe him or not isn't quite clear, but she raised her foot and kicked Bill, together with the bucket and stool, down into the gutter.

Just as he was recovering from this ordeal, Reg Evans appeared in the cowshed and asked what the trouble was.

"Boss, if you want that bloody cow milked, milk the bugger yourself, for I ain't going to touch her again!"

The Boss, not being a man to shirk any job, promptly got bucket and stool, and went to sit down and milk this cow himself. But before he even sat down, she had speedily transferred him to the same gutter, by the same method. Luckily there were a few young calves on the farm at that time, and this cow had made herself so unwelcome in the cowshed by now, that it was decided that it would be much safer to use her for suckling these calves than allowing her to upset the cowshed routine.

Even when she was shut into a loose box with the calves she tried to kick hell out of them, but these three strong animals hung on and eventually managed to suckle her out twice a day. I have had to deal with several awkward animals since then, but that being my first encounter with one will always be the most memorable.

My day would start at six o'clock each morning and finish at six in the evening, except during haymaking when it extended sometimes to 10 o'clock. The Boss and Arthur, after milking two or three cows, left Bill and I to complete the milking and would set off on the milk rounds and return about midday. My chores, after helping muck out and wash down the cowshed each morning, were to lend a hand with whatever needed to be done.

Like most of the dairy farms in that area, the winter diet would be hay, kale, mangolds and, at the Valley, British Oil and Cake Mills (BOCM) dairy cake, delivered weekly in 1½cwts Hessian sacks. The marrow stem kale was usually finished by about the turn of the year, and from then until turnout time mangolds (wurzels) were fed. Being on light, sandy loam soil enabled the cows to go out for about six hours daily, and this was when the kale was fed in the pastures. One of my jobs was to cut and cart this kale. On a dry, crisp winter's day this was quite a pleasant job, but there were many days when it was wet and miserable and I could have described them quite differently. The horse power on this farm amounted to two massive Shire horses, that had spent all their prime years as dray horses in the city of Birmingham, and then been sold off to spend their last years on live stock farms, where the work was fairly light. It was one of these horses, Captain, that I used for kale-carting all the time that I worked at the Valley, and what a great character he was. He was very light grey and had a magnificent mane and well-feathered legs, and must have been the pride and joy of the lucky dray man who had the privilege of driving him.

My job was to cut the very large stalks of kale, up to four feet high, and throw them up into the cart. Captain would always take a step backwards at a command, thus enabling me to get them up into the cart without too much effort. When I had the cart full it was taken out into one of the pastures and, with Captain walking at a steady pace, I would pull the stalks out into a row, ready for consumption by the cows the following morning. Two pastures were always in use for this operation and were used on alternate days, thus allowing the kale to be distributed unhindered by lots of hungry cows.

The mangolds were fed whole each morning. Some farmers were

reluctant to feed their cows in this manner for fear of them choking on them, but in the years that I worked there we never experienced this problem. Hay was fed three times daily throughout the winter with the last feed about 10.00pm.

Each winter all the cows had their flanks, udders and tails clipped, so that they could be kept in stalls. This operation greatly helped in keeping them clean. In those pre-war years bedding straw was difficult to come by in the area around the Valley Farm and peat moss was used with great success for bedding down the stalls. The use of this material was quite simple, a wheel barrow was pushed along with a couple of handfuls thrown into each stall - sufficient to keep the cows very clean. Along with the clipping this made it quite a simple job to brush their flanks before each milking. The peat moss was delivered ex.Great Western Railway (GWR) in bales weighing about 2cwts - not all that easy to handle - no mechanical loaders on the farms in those days!

Another job that mostly fell my way was the washing of the milk bottles and churns that would arrive back off the milk rounds about midday. In my early days at the Valley this was done with a hand brush and a trough of hot water, with each bottle having to be rinsed in cold water. I used to find this a very tedious job as there were several hundred of them each day. It came as a great relief one day when Reg Evans informed me that he had bought an electric bottle washer. This machine made the job quite a bit more acceptable. All these bottles, plus the other dairy equipment, had to be steam-sterilised each day. The steam was generated from a coke-fired boiler which was situated in a small shed adjacent to the dairy.

Lighting the fire was another of my tasks, and had to be timed to get the steam up in time to sterilise all the equipment in readiness for the afternoon milking at 4.00pm. Most times I got it about right, but occasionally the pressure would rise to its maximum before the washing was complete, and set off the safety release valve. Now this valve, when brought into operation, created a high whistling sound with lots of steam escaping and causing quite a fog. With the boiler house being close to the farmhouse this situation soon aroused the attention of Mrs Evans, who was of rather a nervous disposition. On hearing this noise she would think that the boiler was about to explode and come tearing out to the farmyard calling for help. Mostly, this help was quickly available, but on one memorable occasion I had gone with Bill, the cowman, to fix some wire fencing in one of the further meadows. Now Bill, being a very astute countryman, had eyes like a hawk, and was quick to observe any sudden change in the immediate scenery. We were getting on with our work in a steady manner when, all of a sudden, he said, "Stan, you'd better bugger off back to the farm a bit on the quick side, as there be the missus waving like mad, and I think it's not only the bloody boiler that is about to blow off!"

When I started work at Easter in 1937 the wage for a mature farm worker was 30 shillings for a five-and-a-half-day week. For a 14-year-old boy it was 10 shillings, and that is the wage that I received. Five shillings of that was deducted for my full board, lodging and clothes washing. For that amount I worked from 6am to 6pm each day, with maybe an hour or two off midday on a Saturday and Sunday - if I was lucky. On attaining the age of 15 in January 1938 my wage was increased to six shillings a week, but alas, that was the age that I had to start paying National Insurance stamps and promptly had a deduction of four pence per week.

Before the use of artificial insemination in dairy cattle became common practice, natural service was the one and only means of getting the cows back into calf. During my time at the Valley, the bull-in-residence was a rather handsome roan Dairy Shorthorn. Most days he would be turned out with the herd where he would promptly attend to any cows that needed his urgent services. On some occasions, when a more restricted breeding plan was called for, he was kept in his pen, and used only on selected cows.

One morning, one of these cows was kept in her stall to await her turn to be taken round to the bull pen. This day happened to be the very day that Bill had taken a few hours off work to attend to a sick parent. He told me to leave this cow where she was, and he would see to her on his return to work in the afternoon. Thinking that I would do him a good turn, I took the cow around to the yard where the bull pen was situated, let the bull out and he performed his duty in just a few minutes. After getting the bull back into his pen, I was feeling quite pleased with the ease of the operation.

Alas, things began to go very wrong when I began to take the cow back to her stall. The farm buildings were built on two levels, and the cowshed was on the lower one, the roof of which was just a couple of feet off the high level. For some reason, she must have decided that the quickest way back was over the tiled roof. Without too much effort, she managed to leap onto the roof. Although the building was of very sound construction, the roof was only intended to keep the weather out, not to support wayward animals. I ran down to the lower yard, and into the cowshed, expecting to find this poor cow fallen right through the roof and badly injured. Not a bit of it. There she was, suspended safely above my head, with two rafters supporting her body and her four legs dangling in mid-air. What a situation for a 15-year-old boy to sort out.

Knowing that the Boss and my brother Arthur would be back off their milk rounds about midday, I consoled myself to await help. On their arrival back at the farm, to be told that I had got a cow up on the cowshed roof, I was considered a bit of a wag, until they saw for themselves. With the aid of a wagon rope and a bit of muscle power we were able to get her free from her lofty perch. Apart from a few minor scratches she was fine, but the roof needed a dozen fresh tiles to be replaced.

During the summer and autumn months, we used to take the dry cows to a pasture at Dodford, a distance of two miles from the farm. These were looked at daily by whoever happened to be doing the milk round in that area. When any of these cows calved, the task of bringing them back to the farm was often allocated to me. This involved driving the pony and float over to the field, picking up the calf, putting it into the back of the float and closing the door. The mother was always quite willing to follow us on foot; as the float was a very low-slung vehicle, she was able to see and smell the calf, and followed quite happily. Only once did this journey cause me quite a bit of distress. About halfway between the collection point and the farm was an area of market garden crops. As I was driving past this point, with the calf laying down on the floor of the float, my attention must have wavered, for as I glanced round to see that all was well with the cow following, alas, she wasn't in sight! After turning the pony and trap around and driving back in the direction from whence we had come, I spotted a gang of women frantically waving their arms and, in the midst of them, was the cow. These women were engaged in the cutting of cauliflowers. The cow, being much more observant than I was, had spotted the open gate, walked into the field and drawn the attention of these poor ladies. The only way out of this situation was for me to drive out into the field and hope for the cow to regain interest in her calf. This she did, and with a bit of assistance from the women, we got back onto the road to the farm without any further problems.

The next week in the local market, my Boss became engaged in a discussion with the owner of this vegetable field about the stupidity of his boy, driving a pony and float over the cauliflowers, but I understand that with a couple pints of free ale at the market tavern, all was forgiven.

The first tractor that was used at the Valley Farm was a 1926 model Austin. In spite of its age, it had not done a great deal of work before the Boss bought it at a farm sale for £18 early in 1938. The main task for this tractor was to pull the new grass mower that had replaced the old horse mower that had been used for a good many years, and was well in line to be laid up.

This tractor had been made before the days of pneumatic tyres, and was fitted with spade lugs to the wheels. Several meadows of mowing grass had been bought in the locality but we couldn't use this tractor to go from one to another on the road with iron spade lugs. Eventually, we managed to get some solid wheels from a scrapped steam wagon, cut them into suitable sizes and bolted them onto the tractor wheels in place of the lugs, thus making the tractor roadworthy.

Hay-making was quite a long, drawn-out affair at the Valley, starting in mid-June and usually not finished until August. The farm carried on average 40 dairy cows and just a few young animals, not very intensive stocking by today's standards, but no nitrogen was used on grassland in the '30s, just an occasional dressing of basic slag. The hay that was made at the farm was carted and stacked in the Dutch barn, but the mowing grass that was bought around the neighbourhood was built into stacks on the fields and carted back to the farm in the winter as required.

These field stacks were made with the use of a One Horse Sweep. When the hay was considered fit to stack, it was horse raked into rows and the sweeping would commence. The sweep was made of wood, was about 10 feet wide and had eight tines which were six feet long. Each one of these tines was fitted with a slightly upwards-curved metal point. The rear consisted of two large backwards facing handles, for the use of the driver. The extra long harness traces were connected to a swivel at each side of the sweep.

Looking back all those years ago I can still visualise my brother Arthur driving Captain, the old grey shire horse over these rows of hay, sweeping it up into huge lumps right up to, and above, the horse's tail. When he had got enough to comfortably drive up to the stack, he would set off and, on getting alongside, would slightly lift the handles, so that the points would stick into the soil and the sweep would completely somersault, leaving the lump of hay intact, and land ready to set off for the next one. It all sounds quite an easy task, but the driver of the horse had to be pretty nimble on his feet, as when he lifted the handles to tip the sweep, he had to keep hold of the driving lines, taking two or three very swift sidesteps to avoid finishing up on top of the lump.

In the days before the elevator became a common implement on farms, the pitch fork was the only means of conveying the hay off the ground onto the stacks, or the wagons. Being young and keen I used to enjoy the job of pitching, and I can honestly say that I never faced very strong opposition to acquire it. It wasn't the most popular of tasks.

One memory of stack-building is still very clear. It was one evening in the summer of 1939 when we had set out, after milking, to clear a five-acre field of hay. All went well, and by sunset a rather smart-looking stack of good hay had been built in the corner of the field. We all went home, proud of the fact that we had completed this operation before darkness had set in. Alas, our pride was very shortlived. The next morning when Bill, the cowman, arrived at work he met the Boss with the words, "That there stack you were in such a bloody hurry to build be over in next field, or biggest part on it!" It had settled unevenly during the night, and the top part of it had fallen over the hedge into the field below. The task of loading it onto wagons, and rebuilding the stack was carried out with far less enthusiasm than the previous evening's work. This stack was thatched and used during the winter.

In the two-and-a-half years between starting work and the outbreak of the Second World War my social life was rather on the limited side. Never having had much of chance to partake in any sports, I was quite pleased to be invited to join the young social club at Catshill Church in early 1938. This club consisted of about a dozen teenage boys and girls. It was a completely informal club without any set rules, only the ones that were made as and when they were thought necessary!

On Sunday evenings, after most of us had attended evening service, we set off on a stroll to different parts of the parish, mostly in two or three groups. Some evenings we would get invited into a member's home for tea and cakes. Once or twice a week, a few of us would meet up and go to the cinema in Bromsgrove. In those days public transport was much superior to what it is today. We could get a bus every half hour, with the last one leaving town at 11.00pm. We had two cinemas to choose from, and each one changed their programmes twice weekly. Seats cost six pence, nine pence or a shilling, I don't seem to have ever been inclined to go for the higher-priced one.

Every Tuesday and Thursday evening during the summer months, the Rector kindly let us use his grass tennis court. This is where I was first able to play the game, which I got to enjoy, but alas, I never did achieve a very high standard of play. During the haymaking season it wasn't always possible to get away, as work had to come first. Each Tuesday and Thursday at about 6pm, I would offer up a little prayer and ask for a heavy shower of rain - just enough to put a stop to work for the evening without harming the hay, but not sufficient to stop the tennis!

Sometimes my prayer was answered, enabling me to get away to join the gang. In addition to the use of the tennis court, the Rector didn't frown on us if we took shelter in his coach house from the rain. These enforced breaks from the tennis were never completely unfruitful as quite a bit of dating was achieved on these occasions!

Most of the members of this set of friends went on to serve in the various Armed Forces during World War Two. I had the good fortune to meet up with several of them in different areas during my time in the Royal Navy.

On 27th April 1938 Mother became seriously ill with diabetes, just six months after selling our house at Abbeydore and moving into a small bungalow in the suburbs of Worcester. She stayed for two weeks in a nursing home, but sadly spent her last few days in the Worcester Royal Infirmary where she died whilst in a coma.

She was buried alongside my Father in the church yard at Stanford-On-Teme on 25th May. She had not enjoyed the best of health since Father's death in 1934. The whole family were very saddened by her early death at the age of 52 years.

My eldest sister Mary, who was married and lived in Worcester, became the unofficial guardian to the younger members of the family and treated us with loving care for all the years that we needed it.

My brother Frank had applied to join the RAF as flying crew on leaving school and had been accepted. However, on entry, he failed the medical exam due to faulty vision and was discharged - much to his great disappointment. Aunt Amy, Mother's youngest sister, then offered him a home with her family at the Grapes Hotel in Basingstoke and, after spending a few weeks with them, he joined the Royal Army Ordnance Corps (RAOC) and, eventually, he volunteered to join the Indian Army, in which he served for the next 10 years.

Jennie was just 13 at this time and spent two years at the Alice Otley School in Worcester, during which time she lived with sister Mary. On leaving school at 15 she went to work as a children's nurse and, at the age of 18, joined the Women's Auxiliary Air Force (WAAF) for the duration of the War.

Looking back to those faraway days and to losing both my parents at such an early age, I can well remember many happy little incidents that took place in that period of time. One that will always be remembered as one of the proudest took place when I was about nine years old. Unlike today, when warts are very rarely seen, they were quite in evidence in those days, and the one that grew on my left knee was the cause of a bit of teasing on the part of some of the other boys at school. In those days it was unheard of for boys under the age of 14 to wear anything other than short trousers, so no way could I camouflage this ugly ¾inch extension to my left knee. Mother became aware of this discomfort, and one evening she harnessed Kit to the trap and we set off; me sitting proudly beside her as the only other occupant, which I think was about the first time that I had ever been so honoured. On arriving at the doctor's surgery at Bromyard, a small market town seven miles distance from our farm, Kit was tied up in the yard and I was taken in to see Dr Russell. He had a quick look at this offending limb, reached for a pair of scissors and, with one neat cut, off came my wart. A piece of plaster was stuck over the small wound and the doctor said, "Take him home, Mrs Lane, he'll be alright." To be honest, I was a little disappointed at the speed with which this bit of butchery took place. I was hoping to have more of a dramatic story to tell my mates regarding its disappearance, considering the interest they had shown in it for some time!

In the times before my parents bought their first, and only, car in 1931, they relied entirely on the pony and trap for all their social and farming business trips, which included journeys to Church and, during the winter months on a Friday evening, an outing to the whist drive in the Village Hall at Stanford. Occasionally, they would venture a little further and attend one at Upper Sapey. I well remember Mother warming several bricks on the kitchen-fire hob and placing them in the trap to warm her feet during those wintry trips to the Village Hall.

Group of tennis players from the Catshill Church Social Club

62

5. The Valley Farm In Wartime

During the summer of 1939 rumours of War became the main topic of everyday talk. During the evening of Friday 1st September the Boss suggested we look at a small field of oats to see if they were ready to cart and stack. On arriving at the field, which was at the higher part of the farm, with quite a clear view over towards the Austin motor works at Longbridge and beyond, we could hardly believe our eyes, as about 25 massive balloons were suspended several hundred feet up in the sky. The sight of these barrage balloons - which is what they were - confirmed all the talk of the expectation of War. I was 16 years of age.

On Sunday morning of 3rd September I was washing milk bottles in the farm dairy, when I was called over to the farm house by Mrs Evans. An important announcement was to be broadcast on the radio at 11.00am, and would I like to hear it? The Prime Minister, Mr Neville Chamberlain, spoke to the nation and told us that as a result of Germany failing to respond to the ultimatum sent to them by the British Government the previous day, a state of War now existed between the two countries. This statement didn't come as any great shock as we had all become aware of the trouble that had been brewing in Europe.

At the immediate outbreak of War we at the Valley Farm weren't too badly affected. A total blackout was enforced for the whole country. This was a law that caused a lot of inconvenience, as all the windows in the farmhouse and buildings had to be fitted with some kind of cover to prevent any light escaping. In a way, it was an amusing sight to see the various materials that were brought into use to achieve this blackout. Two layers of Hessian sacks were quite effective on the farm for this purpose, but some of the local cottages were a bit stretched to find enough material, and quite a few items of personal clothing were put to secondary use. I don't think that many present-day garments would have been of great use! Amazingly, when the War was only a few weeks old, thousands of yards of blackout material appeared in the shops, much to the relief of the Air Raid Wardens, who had to enforce the blackout.

One particular day, Arthur and I had been cutting back a very overgrown hedge and had a glorious bonfire with the debris. After evening milking, we went back to the fire to make sure that it was well and truly out. At 2.00am there was a heavy hammering on the farmhouse door. Arthur, being a much lighter sleeper than me, was soon up at the window to see what the noise was about. There stood the village bobby, waving his arms, "Come and put that b...... fire out double quick!" After getting half-dressed, we grabbed a couple of buckets each, filled them with water and set off in the direction of the fire, a good half mile from the farmyard. The wind had got up in the night and ignited the embers, hence the flames that were causing the bobby to get so excited.

By now the four buckets were only partly full, but just enough to put out the fire - or so we thought. The bobby, who was rather full of girth and approaching retirement age, had just arrived at the scene of the fire, puffing away like a steam locomotive. Whether it was the fact that we had put the fire out before he got there and he felt a bit put out, I never knew. Anyway, he suggested quite firmly that we should go back, refill our buckets and make doubly sure that the fire was well and truly out. We completed this exercise about 4.00am, wished the bobby a begrudging goodbye, and returned to bed for another hour. After all, he was only doing his duty.

A few weeks into the War, the Government set up the War Agriculture Executive Committee - the War Ag., as it was commonly called until its disbandment in the 1950s. These committees were selected from some of the leading farmers and landowners in each area, and it was their job to impose, and supervise, the carrying out of certain orders issued from head quarters.

With the threat of our food supplies from overseas being cut off due to enemy action, drastic measures were called for to produce more food from our own farms. As farming had been sadly neglected during the 1920s and '30s, the industry was at a very low ebb at the outbreak of War. Suddenly, farmers felt that they were needed and set about their task with a great sense of urgency.

One of the first incentives was the introduction of a £2 per acre, ploughing-up grant for all grassland. As this was a voluntary arrangement, and as most farm rents at that time were little more than £1 per acre, many thousands of acres of old grass were ploughed in that autumn of 1939 as a result. Most of them were planted to winter and spring cereals and some root crops.

It was after this first bout of enthusiasm that the War Ag. came into its own and got busy visiting farms and offering advice and guidance on what crops they should grow, and the best way to go about it. Now some of the farmers while being rather willing to take advice, were not so willing to obey orders, if they thought differently.

I think the farming industry has a lot to be proud of in the way that it responded to the call to grow more food during those years of our greatest need.

The demand for increased production on the farms also increased the need for more workers to achieve this output. The formation of the Women's Land Army (WLA), in the very early days of the War, became a great asset to the industry in providing much of this labour.

One of these WLA girls came to work at the Valley Farm in October 1939. Her name was Mary Burt, though now her name is Mary Lane, and has been for 57 very happy years. Many thanks to the WLA.

In mid-January 1940 we had one of the heaviest falls of snow on record. It was the cause of a lot of inconvenience on the farm, worst of all being the distribution of milk on the two rounds that had been built up over the years. The very narrow roads around the farm had been dug out of sandstone and were several feet below the surface of the surrounding fields. These were completely filled with snow on the morning after the storm. After morning milking was completed, Captain was hitched to the cart which we loaded with the crates of milk, plus a few shovels to help clear a way down the lane. After an hour we arrived down at Catshill School and started to serve the milk to anyone who had been able to get that far. The next day, not having being able to get any empty bottles, the milk had to be carried in churns and measured out into what ever containers our customers could find. This situation lasted several days before the delivery vans were able to travel on the partly cleared roads. It was six weeks before they were able to get to the area around the Lickey Hills.

I have one sad memory of this winter. One of my jobs was to take a couple of trusses of hay out to five 1½-year-old heifers that were being out-wintered in a field at the back of the farm. One morning, only four of them turned up for their feed. I didn't have far to look for the missing one, as I soon found her standing in a deep drift, stone dead and frozen stiff. She stayed there in her frozen state for six weeks and, after being hauled down to the pig sties, was cut up, boiled and used for pig feed.

At the time of the evacuation of the British Army from Dunkirk early in June 1940 the Local Defence Volunteers Force (later to become the Home Guard), was set up. There was an immediate response from men of all ages over 18 (I don't think there was a maximum age limit, not even for Mr Godfrey of *Dad's Army*!). They all joined out of an act of patriotism to help protect the country in the face of an invasion that was expected, but never came.

My brothers Arthur and Syd were quick to join. Brother Frank was already serving in the Army in India, and sister Edith had joined the Queen Alexandra's Nursing Service and went on to serve in North Africa. My youngest sister Jennie was later to serve in the WAAF. I, being only 17 at the formation of the Home Guard, was a little bit peeved at Arthur's response when I suggested to him that I brought my birthday forward a few months to enable me to join him in the ranks. No way was he going to have his younger brother being dishonest and that was that! I did eventually join in January 1941 and stayed until I joined the Royal Navy in the following November.

The platoon of which I became a member used to meet most weekends to train. The sergeant in charge of us was a retired Police Sgt. and a little past his use-by-date, but he did his best. Most the men in our group were either farmers, farm workers or Austin car factory workers, and at that time were all working long hours. Our platoon consisted of 10 men, and one evening each week we used to muster one hour before sunset and remain on duty until sunrise.

Our meeting place was in an old barn very close to The Park Gate Inn, which was more than convenient to get a drink prior to the start of a night's vigil. We patrolled in pairs, on mostly three-hour stints, and then returned to the shelter of the barn for a couple of hours. Our job was to keep a sharp lookout for any enemy airmen who may have had to bail out of their damaged aircraft, or any other unusual activities. In the few months that I served in the Home Guard nothing exciting happened in our four-square miles of territory.

Our neighbouring platoon had a bit of fun one night. The Austin motor works, which by 1941 had become a major aircraft production unit, was an important target for the enemy bombers. This particular night, after dropping some bombs on the factory, they had to jettison the rest of them whilst escaping from the anti-aircraft barrage. Unfortunately, one of these bombs fell in the garden of one of the cottages in the village of Bournheath. This area was well known for its cottage pig-keeping tradition, practically every cottage in this village boasted one or two pigs that were fattened up for consumption by the family. The householders were able to draw extra pig-feed rations from the MAFF to supplement the usual kitchen scraps. This wayward bomb fell and exploded on one of these pig sties, rather disturbing the peaceful slumbers of the two occupants, who were getting close to the time when they would be providing the morning rations for the two families who were their joint owners. The pig that fell into the bottom of the crater was not too much of a problem, as being in a hole, a good 12 feet deep, the owners were able, with the help of a ladder, to keep him fed until a makeshift pen was erected for him. His pen-mate didn't fare so well. He escaped falling into the crater and must have made a speedy escape. The Home Guard were alerted and spent the remainder of their night patrol searching for this pig, but with no luck. He was found, two days later, living quite happily in a field of potatoes.

Through the long spring and summer months of 1941, in spite of the fact that I was now a member of the Home Guard, and working very long hours on the farm, I became a little unsettled. Most of the men of my age group had either volunteered, or had been conscripted into one of the Armed Services. Each day, the BBC news would bring reports of progress, or the lack of it, on the way that the War was going. The battle of Crete was concluded with the Allied Armies, under overwhelming odds, being evacuated to North Africa to join up with our forces that were already located there. The Battle of the Atlantic was being waged with great ferocity with both sides suffering severe losses. The search for, the chase, and ultimately, the sinking of the mighty German battleship, the *Bismarck*, on 27th May, kept the whole nation on tenterhooks. The British fleet had suffered considerable losses in the run-up to this historical event. The greatest of these losses was the sinking of the battle cruiser, HMS Hood, which went down leaving only three survivors out of a complement of over 1,600 men.

Upon hearing this sad announcement on the news, I decided that I would volunteer to join the Royal Navy (RN). Making this decision was quite easy, but carrying it out was fraught with problems. By now, at the great age of 18, I was considered an important member of staff at the Valley Farm. On telling my Boss of my decision to join up, he was quite sad that I would be leaving and asked if I would consider staying on until the autumn to see the haymaking and harvest safely gathered. This I agreed to do. By this time in 1941 greater demands were being made on the farming industry to produce more and more of our own food.

The situation called for more workers who came mostly from the WLA, by now a very important part of the industry. They were engaged in all types of jobs on the farms and were a great credit to the fair sex. The majority came from our cities and adapted themselves readily to country life. Many stayed on after the War and settled into farming, making a great success of it.

I am thinking of Mary who has been a great support to me all our married life. My post-War farming career wouldn't have been so pleasant without her help and, later on, without the aid of our daughters.

All agricultural workers were strictly in a reserved occupation and were ineligible for conscription into the Armed Forces. This situation created a problem for me; how was I to overcome it? The answer came by telling the Chief Petty Officer (CPO), in charge of the recruiting office in Worcester, a white lie. On him asking me for my occupation, I told him that I was a farm worker on a retail dairy farm.

"Now young man, you should well know, that I can't accept any recruits from anyone in a reserved occupation", was the reply I received.

I had expected this comment and was ready with my answer: "Most of my time is taken up with washing dirty milk bottles and other dairy work, a job that could be carried out easily by one of the Land Girls."

This answer seemed to satisfy him, and he duly told me that he would put me onto the register of Royal Navy Recruits. On asking how long it would be before I should expect my calling-up papers, he replied about three weeks. Two days after my interview an official letter arrived in the post (below), On His Majesty's Service, informing me that I must report at HMS Collingwood, Fareham, Hampshire, on 5th November 1941. A railway warrant was included in the letter, along with the times of the trains and connections that I should need to get to my first RN posting.

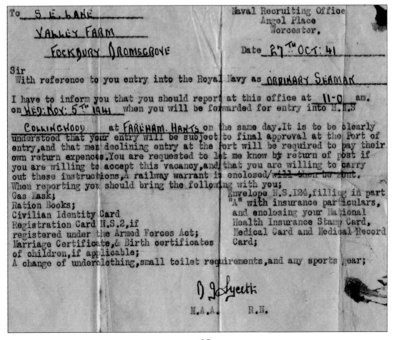

Mary horse-raking during her first year in the WLA

6. Naval Life Begins

HMS Collingwood was the seaman training camp that served the whole of the Portsmouth division of the RN, 6,000 ratings would be training there at any one time. It was here that I arrived, along with several hundred other men on the evening of Guy Fawkes Day, 1941. We were formed into lines, counted off into groups of 24, and a CPO or Petty Officer (PO) took charge of a group and marched it off to a hut which would be home for the time at Collingwood. PO Brooks took charge of the group of which I became a member. He had joined the RN as a boy-seaman at the age of 15, serving 30 years before his retirement. At the outbreak of War he, along with many other men of his rank, were called up, out of reserve, to take part in the training of Hostilities Only ratings. He was an excellent instructor, very strict, but kindly, and spent many hours telling us stories of his time on active service, including service on HMS Lion at the Battle of Jutland, and his four years spent on the China station in the 1920s.

Of the 24 men in our class, only two of us were country-bred, the rest were all from the towns, with the vast majority coming from London - a place I had never seen. We both endured a bit of ribbing from these city dwellers, but after a couple of weeks we managed to give as good as we got (or almost).

The first and only time that I ever got any form of punishment during my time in the RN happened two weeks after my arrival. There were 6,000 trainees at Collingwood, divided into four divisions. Each division had its own mess deck and, like all other operations, the entry into here was carried out with great precision. Each class was marched there at meal times and deposited in an exact place of seating, amongst the other 1,500 ratings in our division. On this particular morning, one of the boys complained of feeling unwell, which was quite understandable as on the previous day we had all had a Typhoid Anti-Bacterial (TAB) jab, and after-effects were common. He asked PO Brooks if he could be excused going on breakfast parade as he didn't feel he could eat anything. This request was granted and he was told to stay put. On sitting down to our breakfast the class were faced with a problem, only 23 men to consume 24 breakfasts which were already laid out on our table. No way was that spare breakfast going to find its way back to the galley.

The three of us sitting next to the vacant seat decided that it was our duty to avoid this happening, and disposed of it with relish. Feeling rather pleased with ourselves for getting a larger breakfast than usual, we were slightly disturbed to see this sick classmate come into the mess deck and take his seat next to us. In answer to his question as to the whereabouts of his breakfast he wasn't at all pleased to be told that we had eaten it. In spite of us telling him that we were under the impression that he was too unwell to eat it himself, he reported the loss of it to the duty PO, who called us out, and duly marched the three of us to meet the officer of the watch on duty. He happened to be rather a pompous, young Royal Naval Volunteer Reserves (RNVR) Lieutenant and he made a lengthy inquiry into which of us had eaten the bacon and which the bread. My only crime was to have consumed the full half ounce of butter, which happened to be the daily allowance at that time. At the end of this enquiry we were stood out in front of the whole 1,500 men, and the Lieutenant expounded on the wickedness of stealing a shipmate's breakfast. The four days' punishment that he bestowed on us turned out trumps for us. We had to report to the galley each night and the duty chief cook would give us each a couple of hours' work, peeling potatoes and carrots. At the end of each session we were rewarded with a real slap-up meal, much envied by the rest of the class, including the boy who had lost his breakfast!

After 10 weeks' basic training at Collingwood we were drafted to various other specialist training courses. I was drafted to HMS Vernon, the main torpedo school in Portsmouth, where I spent a short while awaiting my next move.

A couple of weeks before leaving Collingwood, an Engineer Officer addressed us, and asked if any of us would care to become Engine Room Mechanics (ERM). The RN was desperately short of Engine Room Artificers (ERA) and were looking for unskilled men to volunteer to be trained and help fill this shortfall. On completion of a six-month training course we would become ERMs and work alongside ERAs, the professional engineers. Along with two other men from my class I put my name forward and we were accepted to go on this course.

This decision was one that I regretted for the whole time I served in the RN, the reason for which will become apparent as I continue to brief you with my naval career.

In mid-January 1942, 40 of us were sent up to Wallsend-on-Tyne to start our engineering course at a civilian Government training centre. We were all to be billeted in private lodgings, under a compulsory billeting order that was imposed on the residents in that part of the country. A coach met us at Newcastle Station, and the driver had a list of addresses and the number of men to be dropped off at each one. After letting off several at houses in the back streets we came into the main street and stopped in front of No.49, High Street, Wallsend-On-Tyne. The next six were dropped off in the front of this three storey house, me being one of them. Mrs Kirkwood, the landlady met us at the door and told us to put our kit bags and any other luggage down in the hallway, as she would like a few words with us before settling in. These few words turned out to be a comprehensive list of house rules that she would expect to be observed without question. We were to be her first lodgers under the compulsory scheme, and she wasn't too pleased at having to accommodate us for the huge sum of 16 shillings a week, and provide us with bed, breakfast and an evening meal seven days a week. She already had five long-standing lodgers who were paying twice that amount.

My three months living in that household is a period that I will never forget. The two upper floors consisted of four bedrooms and a bathroom that was shared by the whole household of 14 inmates. The basement contained the living kitchen, scullery and coal house. The kitchen contained a large, old-time cooking range which was the only means of heat for the whole household. A wash boiler was situated in the scullery, which was lighted twice a week for the benefit of the civilian lodgers to get baths. We naval ratings weren't allowed this privilege as it was considered that 16 shillings-a-week payment didn't warrant the luxury of baths. We did get a free pass to use the council baths for the time we spent at Wallsend.

The large kitchen was the life centre of all the occupants; containing a large table and a dozen chairs, and shelves which supported all kinds of food stuffs for the use of all the guests. It also had a bed in one corner which was occupied by Davy, the landlord. Davy had suffered a severe stroke and had been bedridden for a couple of years. Although he was incapable of speech, the sight of us in naval uniforms entering the room seemed to cheer him up a lot; as a young man he had served for seven years in the RN and the sight of us must have revived his memory. Also, in view of the fact of having six extra lodgers thrust upon her, Mrs Kirkwood and her 18-year-old daughter had to sleep on the hearth rug in front of the range fire.

This daughter was the subject of one of the house rules that had been read out to us on arrival. She was already married and her husband was away at sea, serving in the Merchant Navy. No way were we to get too familiar with her, or we would have a lot to answer for. She was a pretty

72

girl, but had a fiery temper which was put to full use at times, especially if any of the lodgers happened, on coming down early to breakfast, found her semi-clad and still in the midst of her morning toiletry.

Gas was the only means of lighting the house and, for reasons of economy, the mantles had been removed from all the bedroom lights to deter anyone from reading in bed. This situation was the cause of quite a delicate bit of timing on the part of Mrs Kirkwood each morning. On the top floor slept Beck, one of the six civilian lodgers, and being on early shift meant he had to have a wake-up call each morning. With the absence of lighting on any of the upper floors, the landlady would make a good twist of several sheets of newspaper and stick it into the fire to get it well alight. With a great turn of speed, she would ascend the stairs, go into the top bedroom, give Beck a hefty shake and be back down in the kitchen with the paper still alight. Being used to early mornings, I was always awake to see this streak of lightning pass by my door on the way to the floor above.

One morning the landlady designated this job to the daughter, and this happened to be the morning that Beck had woken early and was out on the landing, about to call and ask the time. The young lady, with her torch well alight got to the foot of the stairs, looked up and saw this face peering down at her. She turned tail and ran back into the kitchen, screaming, "Mum, Mum, there's Beck up there, trying to hang his self over the banisters!"

"Well, let the bugger hang his self, we can soon find another lodger!" was her instant reply.

Our evening meal didn't quite come up to the luxury of the present-day McDonalds takeaway. Each evening, round about 7 o'clock, Mrs Kirkwood would grab whichever boy happened to be in her way, give him 26 pence, and send him to the fish and chip shop that was almost next door. The order was 13 two pennyworth of chips to be put into 13 separate packs, sufficient for all the lodgers, plus the two ladies of the house. Whichever member of the household was designated to get this rather large order was provided with a large, old wicker wash basket to collect it in. On entering the chip shop, and the chippy seeing this basket, he would call out to his wife: "13 tuppenceworth and give 'em good weight, the poor buggers must be in need of it!"

These packs, complete with their newspaper wrapping, were put into the oven to be kept warm. Whatever time the lodger felt fit for his supper, he took out one of these packs, and made the most of what was his complete evening meal - except for a mug of rather well-brewed tea that was always kept warm on the hob. I will always remember the very large, brown, enamel pot from which this tea was poured. Each morning, this pot was emptied of the previous day's remains and replenished with several spoons of tea (this was before the days of tea bags). As the day wore on, more spoons of tea and more water were added and, by the end of the day, it nearly needed the help of a spoon to get it out of the pot!

One of Mrs Kirkwood's favourite hobbies was arguing with her neighbours and, most afternoons, on arriving back at the lodgings we boys had to hear all about which one of them had been unlucky enough to have crossed her path that morning. In the excitement of telling us all about the build-up to these confrontations, we would hear all about this particular neighbour's lifestyle and their ancestry, which in some cases was of suspect accuracy. She had a very broad Geordie dialect that was a joy to the ear, but in times of excitement it became rather difficult to follow her drift. This daily bulletin of 'life with the neighbours' was looked on as quite an entertainment for us ratings on our return from the training centre each day. After a while, we started to lay bets on which one was to play the leading role in that day's episode, as by now we were familiar with most of the cast of this 1940s version of *Coronation Street*.

Although Wallsend was close to the Durham coalfields, coal seemed to be in very short supply, especially at No.49. The weekly ration was delivered each Monday morning, but by the extravagant use of it in that kitchen range, the ration was mostly used up by Friday, and that is where the naval lodgers became Mrs Kirkwood's blue-eyed boys - just for the day! On our return from training, she would ask us to go into town and plead with any coalman who was delivering from his pony and cart to sell us a bag of coal. We were always successful in getting at least one bag, and when this extended to two, the good lady was in raptures, as she was assured that now she could keep her Davy in the warmth that he deserved.

One week of extra cold weather had resulted in the stock of coal being exhausted a day earlier than usual. This situation became apparent on our sitting down to a cup of tea at the kitchen table. Two chairs were missing, and on asking Ma where they were, she replied that being at her wits end to find enough fuel to keep Davy warm, she had broken them up and used them on the range fire. One of the boys, being a bit of a wit, readily suggested we went up into the one bedroom which housed a piano which was never used, break it up and bring it down to the kitchen for fuel. This suggestion didn't go down at all well, but on him offering to go down town and try to get a sack of coal all was forgiven! The six of us set off and an hour later we got back to the lodgings with three bags full, much to the delight of Mrs Kirkwood.

Each of these sacks of coal (weighing 1cwt) had to be carried on our backs; no problem to me but a couple of the lads who had never carried anything heavier than their kit bags were the cause of a lot of jovial remarks from the street walkers, as they were seen struggling along bent double. We more able navvies soon relieved them of their misery.

During the 12 weeks that I spent at the training centre I was instructed in fitting, turning, welding and had become familiar with quite a lot of engineering practices (or so I thought). My mechanical skills were very restricted before going on this course, so on leaving I was more than pleased to be described in my report as a good worker who should go on to make a satisfactory ERM after completing my training.

From Wallsend, we were transferred to a similar centre at Pontefract in Yorkshire, where we completed the final 12 weeks of our training. Having just got to understand the Geordie dialect, I found the Yorkshire accent much easier but just as fascinating. My lodgings in Laburnam Avenue were a

Stan, ERM, 21 years old

complete contrast to the ones in the High Street, very sedate and hosted by an elderly couple, who treated us three boys with loving care.

On leaving Pontefract in June 1942 with a grade B pass, I went back to RNB at Portsmouth and acquired the rank of Probationary ERM. At last I was going to join a ship and begin the job for which I had joined Navy. On returning from a week's leave, to my utter disappointment, a draft chit was awaiting me, instructing me to report to the drafting office with my kit bag and hammock the following morning at 0900 hours, en route to HMS Hornet, a shore base at Gosport, just across the water from Portsmouth. It was at this establishment that I spent the most boring 12½ months of my life.

7. Service In The Royal Navy

HMS Hornet was one of the main bases of the coastal service, sheltering motor torpedo boats, motor gunboats, motor launches and other light coastal craft.

Apart from being an operational base, a lot of the major repair and maintenance work was carried out here. After 200 hours of running, the engines from these craft were removed and taken into the massive workshop in what was called Gun Boat Yard. Three makes of engine were serviced, the British Thorneycroft, the American Packard and the Italian Isotta Fraschini. It was on this latter that I worked for 13 months of my service time. On arrival at the workshop each engine was completely stripped down, and the various parts moved on to the department that dealt with them. By this time in 1942, with Italy having been on the enemy side for the past couple of years, the spares for these Isotta engines were no longer available. Unless they could be made in the workshop the engines were gradually being taken out of commission, to the dismay of the boat crews, as the Isotta engine was much in favour with its superior speed.

Each of these engines contained 18 cylinders, in three banks of six cylinders. Each of these cylinders contained four valves, making a total of 72 for each engine. It was amongst these valves that I spent months of extreme boredom. I became a member of the three-part-valve grinding team, whose sole job was to grind these wretched little things to a state of perfection, before the chief mechanic gave them his approval. The cylinder heads would arrive at our section with the valve seats already having been machined. Our job was to get a round stick which had a rubber sucker attached to the end of it, stick it onto a valve head, apply some carborundum paste to the valve face and start grinding. This exercise consisted of using the palms of both hands to twiddle the stick and apply gentle pressure, and after one, two, three hours and very often all day, the valve was passed as being satisfactory for use.

I expect, by now, the reader will be bored with hearing about engine valves, but how do you think I felt about them after 13 months of their company? It wasn't quite the contribution to the war effort that I had envisaged on volunteering to join the RN, but thousands of other young men must have suffered similar frustration to me.

The Haslar Royal Naval Hospital adjoined the Hornet, where we were allowed the privilege of using their tennis courts during the summer evenings. Another source of recreation was the unofficial use of some bicycles, which were strictly for the use of the Wrens to travel from their place of residence to their department. Some of these Wrens worked alongside us in the workshops and would, on occasion, consent to letting us use their bikes for the odd evening excursion to Lee-on-Solent and beyond.

All the men had to be back in the base by 11.00pm, except for the monthly dance night at Haslar Town Hall when midnight was the deadline. One of these nights I well remember, a group of us having decided that before we patronised the dance we would go and have a beer or two on our walk down to the hall. Whilst having our first drink at this pub the landlady asked us if we would like to buy a raffle ticket for the draw that would take place at 9.00pm that evening. Each of us five men invested in two sixpenny tickets. Now having all that money at stake we were a bit reluctant to leave the pub before the draw took place, so another round was called for and, by the time 9.00pm arrived, several more rounds had been consumed.

By this time the landlady had become aware that our little group were awaiting the outcome of the raffle, and asked one of the boys to pick the first ticket out of the hat. To my surprise, and pleasure, it was number 58, my ticket. On being invited to go up to the bar to choose my prize, I was confronted with the choice between a bottle of whisky, a box of toffees or a brace of white rabbits. To the dismay of my mates, thinking they were going to get their first taste of whisky, I chose the rabbits. After buying another round, just to pacify them in their disappointment, we set off to the dance, with me carrying the two rabbits. On arrival at the Town Hall, the doorman was a bit reluctant to let me in, as he explained that he wasn't in the habit of allowing dead stock into the dance hall. After informing him that I would hang them up in the cloakroom with my greatcoat covering them, he relented, and let me in.

At a quarter to midnight - time to leave and return to base - I discovered to my dismay that the prize rabbits had disappeared from underneath my greatcoat. Now having had quite a discussion amongst our party as to what to do with these bunnies, several suggestions had been made and in the end it had been decided to present them to Ma Jordan (the PO Wren in charge of our galley), a very kind and homely person; the thinking behind this presentation being that she might be persuaded to make a stew and let our little group share it with her.

With the disappearance of my prize, action was called for, so I hastily returned to base and, after a short time pleading with the Master at Arms, he instructed the guards to search each of the men as they returned for two white rabbits. Now this order being rather a one-off search was the cause of much merriment among the guards, and I think they got more pleasure out of hunting for them than I did winning them. They never came to light, but I rather think they may have got secretly interned in the guard room.

During my 12 months at Hornet we were allowed one weekend leave each month, most of these I spent with Auntie Amy (Mother's youngest sister) at Basingstoke, a 1½ hour bus trip from Gosport. She owned and lived at the Grapes Hotel with Uncle Jack and cousins John and Jean. At that period of time in 1942 and early 1943 many thousands of American troops were stationed in the south of England. Many of these troops used to make their way to the Grapes on their nights off. I was soon roped in to helping behind the public bar, serving various drinks to these very friendly, but rather noisy, troops. Wearing my uniform whilst serving was the cause of many of them insisting that I would take a drink with them; mostly I would slip the money discreetly into the staff gratuity pot, but not always. One particularly busy Saturday evening, the bar being extra crowded and noisy, I had not made sufficient use of the money pot and had accepted their hospitality in liquid form. As the evening progressed so did their thirst, and I was having quite a tussle to keep up with pleas for a refill of their glasses. After the pub was cleared of all its revellers, and having a little time to review the stock behind the bar, I found to my dismay that I had been replacing the empty whisky bottles with bottles of rum! On informing Aunt Amy of this discrepancy, her reply was, "Don't get worried Stan, judging by the happy state of those soldiers they wouldn't know or care which of those two spirits they had been consuming." I did make sure that I didn't repeat the mistake in my subsequent spells of duty as very temporary bar assistant.

After serving for 12 months at HMS Hornet, I was getting quite disillusioned with my role in the War that was now in its fourth year. Some of my fellow men who were of the same opinion as myself volunteered to be drafted to foreign service. A few of us had our requests granted. I was one of the lucky ones, or so I thought... On leaving Hornet and returning to RN barracks at Portsmouth to await this foreign draft four of us ERM 5 (5th Class) joined the Battleship, HMS Queen Elizabeth, which was in dry dock in Portsmouth harbour. She had just returned from major repairs in the port of Norfolk, Virginia in the USA. As a result of being attacked with torpedoes by Midget Italian

Submarines in the Naval base at Alexandria she suffered major damage and was out of commission for about 18 months. Our job was to assist the ERA 5 (5th Class) in carrying out minor repairs before she went back to join the home fleet. At last I was going to sea on one of our capital ships. Imagine my great disappointment, after three weeks on this great ship, to be told that us four ERM 5 were surplus to the ship's full complement and we would be returning to RN barracks. On my return to this establishment I spent a week feeling quite at odds with the Senior Service. This feeling of depression was partly overcome when on the morning of 18th December 1943 I got a draft to HMS Orlando, a shore establishment at Greenock on the River Clyde.

*

The time I spent at this repair dockyard was the most satisfying of my whole time in the RN. We were always kept busy with different tasks on a variety of ships. Most of the ships that we serviced were corvettes and sloops. These sturdy little ships were engaged in the protection of the convoys of merchant ships that were conveying much needed supplies to the northern Russian port of Murmansk. Their main armaments were depth charges which were used very effectively to deter, and some times destroy, any German U Boats that were intent on torpedoing our shipping. These small ships were incapable of great speed, but were fully capable of keeping pace with the merchant ships. The outer defence of the convoys was carried out by the larger and faster battle cruisers and destroyers.

As a ship arrived in the dockyard, the engineer officer in charge of our party would board it and get a full list of necessary repairs from the ship's engineer.

I remember the day HMS Chrysanthemum (one of the flower class corvettes) came into harbour at rather more speed than the Admiralty's instructions specified, with the result that the jetty to which she was destined to tie up got a severe jousting as her bows made rather an ugly dent in the wooden structure.

A couple of hours after she had eventually been safely moored against the damaged jetty our engineer officer, thinking it must be a good time to go aboard and get the list of defects, so that he could put them into effect as soon as possible, invited me to accompany him on his mission. To his dismay, and my amusement, on knocking on the door marked Senior Engineer, there was no response. After a short wait he opened the door to rather a peaceful scene. There slumped at the table was the engineer with his two gold rings on his sleeve. At his side was a part jar of Pusser's Rum and an empty tumbler. The velocity of his snoring indicated that he wasn't in the right mood to discuss his repair list, with the result that my officer turned to me and said, "Lane, we will return in the morning".

Sometimes these small ships would get a severe battering from enemy planes which were making their way out from airfields in the north of Norway. The outcome of such raids resulted in quite a lot of damage to the ships and much stress to the crews. It was from one of these convoy escorts that this corvette was returning to the shelter of the River Clyde. The weather during their several weeks at sea had been atrocious with the result that some of their stores had been badly damaged, including several jars of rum that were smashed. The officer in charge of supplies had the task of making claims for the replacement of all these ruined stores when they returned to port. The Bosu'n in charge of the rum was sometimes a little confused as to the exact number of jars that were broken, but would err on the safe side when making claims for their replacement! The result of these miscalculations enabled this ship's company to celebrate (with a few tots of rum) their safe return from such a hazardous trip.

Much of my work involved the repair of leaking joints on the steam pipe lines that led from the boilers to the engines and other ancillary machinery (fuel and water pumps, generators, etc). Our first job was to remove all of the internal steam feed pipes inside the boilers. This was rather an unpleasant job as it entailed crawling on your stomach to reach some of the joints, all of which had to be opened up. Each joint had four nuts and bolts securing them, and before the nuts could be released a split pin had to be removed from each bolt - not an easy task in a lying-down position. When all this pipe work had been taken out of the boilers a gang of civilian dock workers would enter and descale the whole of the chamber, and a couple of days later ERMs would replace the feed pipes, complete with new joints and split pins.

Often we would be called on to work all through the night to enable one of the corvettes to sail at short notice. Only the minor running repairs were carried out on board these ships by ERMs, the major jobs were the work of the civilian dock yard engineers, who were all highly skilled tradesmen.

It was after one of these hectic, all night working parties that a very embarrassing situation arose with our working party. The previous day one of the steam valves had been taken up to the dockyard workshop to be refaced. This said valve was the only item that was the cause of the corvette not being able to sail at 6.00am that morning. It was only going to take twenty minutes to fit it once it arrived on board. One of our party was waiting in the workshop to bring it straight back to the ship as soon as it was ready. It was with great relief when at 6.15am we saw him coming at a fair speed across the dockyard carrying this valve which weighed about 60lbs. Being of the same frame of mind as the rest of our party, and wanting to get this piece of equipment back on board in good time, he called out as he came alongside the ship, "Take this over the side, it will be much quicker than coming up the gangway!"

So it was, but with disastrous results. This valve was opened and closed with a wheel of about nine inches diameter. The wheel was secured by a nut on the end of the valve stem, but unfortunately it had not been replaced. Being carried with one hand at an angle, the wheel managed to remain in position, until the exchange over the ship's side. As the man on board took hold, the wheel balanced itself and, to our dismay, the two men were left holding the wheel while the valve dropped into six fathoms of water. No way could the ship put to sea without the valve. A diver was called and it was recovered in good time, but still the sailing was delayed until 10.00am.

For most of the time that I was stationed at Greenock I worked alongside a man by the name of Sandy Adamson. He was 20 years my senior and, like me, country-bred. He revelled in talking about the very close community with whom he lived in a small village in the centre of West Lothian. As a boy he had spent the first few years of his working life on a farm in his own village. At the age of 18 he decided that he didn't want to spend all his life mucking out and feeding pigs, tattie picking and all the other lowly jobs that were allocated to the younger members of the farm staff. He managed to get a job as mate on one of the barges that worked on the Caledonian Canal. After a few years in this position in the two-man crew his Captain retired and he took over as the skipper of the barge.

Now Sandy was a very meticulous man in all his ways and he didn't hesitate to point out to me the error of my ways if my work didn't always quite come up to his high standard. When the occasion arose and he decided that there was time for a smoke, out would come his pipe from the top pocket of his boiler suit and a tin of St Bruno from the hidden depths under this garment. The silver cover was removed from the pipe, followed by a few sharp taps to remove the remains of the previous session. The filling of this pipe was quite a ritual; first the lid was removed from the tin and a small amount of tobacco placed in the bottom of the bowl of the pipe which was then tamped down with his fore finger. The operation was repeated until Sandy decided that all was ready for him to light up. Once he was satisfied that the pipe was well ignited he would replace the lid and carry on working, puffing away at his pipe without any hindrance whatsoever. The aroma from the St Bruno will always remind me of the pleasant times I spent working alongside this little Scotsman. I sincerely hope that he was able to go back to skippering his beloved barge at his demob from the Navy.

A number of us acquired nicknames in the time-honoured Navy tradition - if we had a surname which lent itself to improvisation. So it was that I became 'Shady' Lane, and my colleagues 'Chalky' White and 'Dusty' Miller, to name a few.

During the time that I served at Greenock, along with 60 other naval personnel, I was billeted in a civilian community centre on the outskirts of the town. All of our meals were cooked and served by the Women's Voluntary Services - and what a superb job they made of it.

Towards the end of October 1944, with the invasion of Europe well established, the pressure of repairs needed at Greenock was much reduced and several members of our staff were drafted back to RN barracks, Portsmouth, with me being one of them.

Now began another short period of uncertainty as to where my next drafting would be. On my first day back in barracks I went along to the drafting office and put my name down to get a transfer to the Submarine Service and, to my great surprise, 10 days later I was drafted to HMS Dolphin, Gosport, the main submarine base in the UK.

*

At this period of time the War at sea was far less intense than it had been for the previous five years and a lot of our warships were being dispatched to the Far East to join the British Pacific Fleet, in readiness for action against the Japanese. On 16th February 1945 I got a draft to HMS Adamant which was a submarine depot ship. Along with several other ERMs, we were transported back up to the River Clyde and joined the New Zealand ship, MV Orangia, which was moored in the Gare Loch. The convoy that we joined during the hours of darkness was well out of sight of land by first light. The sea was quite rough with 20ft waves and I seem to remember thinking that now, after 3½ years in the RN, I was actually at sea, not a record that I was particularly proud of, but that is the way of the world.

The MV Orangia had been built as a passenger liner in the early '30s and had been commandeered for troop-carrying at the outbreak of War.

The crew was mostly Asian and what an efficient lot of men they were. The ship was kept spotless but my biggest disappointment was the fact that none of us naval personnel were allowed to take any part whatsoever in the working of the ship, even our meals were served up to us in rather a swish dining hall by turbaned Sikh waiters. As this was to be my home until we finally reached our destination my feeling of frustration at this lack of activity was hard to bear.

It was six weeks later that we arrived in Trincomalee, a beautiful, sheltered, inland harbour in the NE area of Ceylon (now Sri Lanka). On our way out we had called at several ports including Alexandria for one night but weren't allowed ashore, and Port Said for nearly a week. The reason for the long stay at the latter was the fact that we had to wait for the Suez Canal to become clear of all shipping before our convoy could continue its journey south. At that time I think that there was quite a bit of anti-British sentiment at large, hence the Egyptian port authorities being a little slow in allowing our convoy to enter the canal.

The only act of violence (or attempted violence) that I encountered during my time in the RN, was not against the common enemy, but against a group of 10 to 12 year-old urchins in a quiet street in Port Said. One day, along with two friends, I went ashore with the idea of having a good look around the city, as this would be the very first time that I had set foot on foreign soil. To be truthful, I wasn't over-impressed with what I saw, everything was scruffy and untidy. We went into a couple of shops but the only purchase was four films for my 120 Kodak Box camera (all of which turned out to be complete duds when presented for development on my return back home).

Shoe-shine boys were in evidence at most of the street corners and the first group of three accosted us with, "I shine your shoes Sir, only two pennies?" The three of us having left the ship with perfectly clean shoes didn't think we needed to take up their offer, and told them so. Had we been more familiar with the customs of these youngsters we would have thrown them a few coins and gone on our way with their thanks, but that wasn't to be. They ran on ahead of us, picking up stones from the roadside and joined up with another gang of boys, a couple of streets ahead, who were engaged in the same profession.

As we went to pass them by on the pavement, they shouted out, "Shoe-shine, Sir?" pointing to our shoes and we replied again, "Our shoes already shine". Then came their answer, "Sir, we shine your shoes or we throw stones at your heads", and by this time every one of them was holding a stone in each hand.

We had gone out just to have a quiet walk in this foreign city and here we were being challenged by a dozen scruffy, bare-footed street urchins, intent on us give into their demands.

Faced with this desperate-looking crowd, and not liking the look of the stones they were aiming at us, we made a quick decision and said, "Okay, you shine shoes!" After they had shone our already bright shoes and been given their few pence, they changed from being an aggressive crowd into a friendly little group and even thanked us for their rewards.

From Port Said we passed through the Canal and into the Red Sea, and on leaving that area the convoy was dispersed, with our ship making its own passage onto Bombay. We stayed here for six days, awaiting an escort to our next port of call which was to be Colombo. During our stay in Bombay we were allowed to go ashore on two separate days, with four hours being the allotted time of our freedom each day.

The first day of our visit we walked around the area adjoining the docks, and I had my first vision of extreme poverty. Many people, both young and old, were sitting or lying in doorways or on the pavements, waiting to be thrown a few coins to help them buy a few scraps of food.

I sincerely hope that now, at the beginning of the new millennium, a way can be found to ensure that the whole of mankind is assured of enough of the good food which nature is so capable of producing.

When we finally arrived at Trincomalee, HMS Adamant - to our dismay - had sailed two weeks before our arrival and was by then in the port of Fremantle, Western Australia. After a few days spent in this very picturesque port we set sail to join our ship. Two days into our voyage we crossed the line and the following morning we were given the news that hostilities in Europe had ceased and all our efforts were to hasten the defeat of the Japanese. At noon that day came the announcement over the tannoy that His Majesty the King had ordered the whole British fleet to 'splice the main brace' (an extra ration of rum).

The daily tot of rum was issued at noon each day whilst in temperate zones, but in tropical zones it was issued at 5.00pm. On enrolling into the R N we had the choice to register as T, G, or UA (Temperance, Grog or Under Age). Any one choosing Temperance received an extra threepence-a-day pay. The UAs, on attaining the age of 20, could change to either T or G. At precisely 5.00pm on this first VE day, came the order over the tannoy: "Splice the Main Brace, all men Under Age and Temperance ratings muster for a double issue of Lime Juice". All rules were cast aside as the Ts and UAs were offered generous 'sippers' from our double tots of rum to celebrate this great day.

A few days after this, somewhere in the middle of the Indian ocean, I had to report to the 'quack' (medical officer). I was suffering with a very sore throat and high temperature. I was given a bed in the sick bay, and the following morning the quack, accompanied by a sick-berth attendant (SBA), paid me a visit at my bedside. The attendant carried a small tray on which was a lighted candle, and a short length of fine wire with a ring at the end of it. The SBA held my mouth wide open and the MO held the wire over the candle for a brief period, pushed it down my throat for a few seconds, withdrew it and the SBA let go of my jaws and said, "Goodbye, you'll be fine in a couple of days!"

The following morning the quack came to see me and in answer to my question as to what he had done to my throat, he replied that he had taken the end off my tonsils. To this day I don't know whether I swallowed the bit of tonsil that he cut off, as I can't recollect anything other than the wire being extracted from my mouth. Whatever the answer, I am grateful for the relief it brought, as I had been troubled by sore throats for years and since then they have been a thing of the past.

At last, on our arrival in Fremantle, we caught up with HMS Adamant which was tied up with Dutch and American submarine depot ships at the same quayside. We transferred to the Adamant and the Orangia sailed on to Sydney with the rest of its passengers. The submarines from this base were patrolling the seas around the Dutch East Indies to track down any Japanese ships operating in that area.

Working with the ERAs was a most interesting job. We would go aboard the various submarines and carry out any minor repairs that were necessary. Any major faults would be undertaken by the civilian dockyard engineers in the one and only dry dock in Fremantle harbour. Some of our time was spent on the Dutch submarines, assisting their engineers with repairs.

While the subs were being serviced, the crews spent their few days' leave at a leisure camp which the Australian nation had built for the benefit of its own and Allied servicemen. It was situated between Perth and Kalgoorlie. By all reports it was a great place to get away from the cramped life aboard a submarine.

In mid-July 1945, seven weeks after I joined the Adamant, she received orders to sail at quite short notice for 'Destination Unknown'. Two days later we were at sea and were informed that we were destined to go to the Marianas, a group of islands in the north-western Pacific Ocean, a distance of over 4,000 miles. Our route was via Sydney where we were to pick up a large amount of anchor cable. We needed this cable because the Mariana Islands lay in one of the deepest parts of the Pacific and, with no docking facilities available, we were to ride at anchor whilst servicing the submarines that were destined to meet up with us at a later date, albeit by a different route.

The reason for our quick departure from Fremantle was the speed at which the War against Japan was progressing. The whole of the Dutch East Indies, the Caroline Islands and several other outlying islands had all been cleared of Japanese invaders. The whole of the American and British Pacific fleets were moving ever closer to the Japanese mainland, with the idea of forcing a complete surrender.

We arrived in Sydney Harbour about 10.00pm on 3rd August. The sight of the Harbour Bridge with all its lights, and the city lights beyond, is something I will remember forever. The next morning we were told that we would be leaving on our voyage four days later.

At last it was in my grasp to catch up with some of my father's family history. The source of this information was to come from Aunt Edith, my late father's sister. My sister Mary had given me her address before I left England just in case I ever chanced to be out in that part of the world.

Walking along the dockside the following afternoon, I asked a dockworker as to the whereabouts of South Hurstville. He greeted me with the words: "You're a lucky bugger, mate! I can take you right to a bloody cobber that lives out that way!" He promptly took me along to meet his cobber and introduced me as a Pommy searching for a long-lost aunt. Being in the region of 10,000 miles away from home, it struck me as being quite a miracle that this very man, whose name was Ben Thompson, was a neighbour of my aunt who lived at 38 Boronia St., South Hurstville, and he lived at No.41 just across the road.

After receiving full guidance on how to get out to their street, I asked him to keep it a secret that a nephew would be calling on her in a very short while. The following afternoon as I stood on her doorstep, awaiting a reply to my knocking, I was feeling a little sad at the thought that I would be the first member of our family to meet up with the Australian branch.

The door opened and there stood Aunt Edith. She took one look at me and said, "You must be Stanley," and gave me a great big hug. My sister Mary had written to her a few weeks previously and told her that I might be somewhere in the Pacific area.

As she spoke these few comforting words her Herefordshire accent immediately reminded me of my father. She called out to Uncle Jack,

"Come out to meet my nephew who has come all the way from England!" He still had a Sussex accent, the county he had left half a century earlier.

I was soon sitting in their parlour and being asked lots of questions about my brothers and sisters. Although my sisters Mary and Edith had corresponded with Aunt Edith and Lizzie (now deceased), she was delighted to have me there to catch up with the family news.

*

A couple of days before we were due to complete our voyage to the Marianas the atomic bombs were dropped on the Japanese cities of Hiroshima and Nagasaki. This situation meant that the end of the War was imminent and our trip to the Marianas was cancelled. Along with all the other ERMs aboard the Adamant I was drafted to HMS Golden Hind, the shore base in Sydney. We were billeted under canvas in an exUS army camp situated in the centre of a racecourse near to the town of Liverpool, about 20 miles from Sydney. Early each morning we had the pleasure of seeing a string of horses taking their morning gallop around the camp.

This extra time enabled me to visit my aunt and uncle on several occasions and on each of my visits I learned a little more family history.

As I have said before Grandfather Lane sailed from England in 1887 and disembarked at the Port of Rockhampton in Queensland in October of that year. He had with him four of his children, Arthur, William, Elizabeth and Edith. After disembarking at Rockhampton Grandfather, along with four young children, set off to Gumloo, a very remote location, situated several miles inland north of Townsville.

At that period of time in the later part of the 19th century the government of the day were making concessions of undeveloped land to anyone considered capable of developing it for farming. The block of land that Grandfather was granted was a half section. Aunt Edith told me a lot about the hard life the family endured in those early years on this new settlement. Grandfather was determined to make a success of this new life, having lost most of his money before he left England.

In 1910, having developed the land and accumulated a little capital, he moved to a less isolated farm near Townsville. This farm was on much better soil and more valuable crops were able to be grown such as pineapples, pumpkins, tomatoes, mangoes and other exotic crops.

On leaving school Aunt Edith and Elizabeth went into private service until they were old enough to go into the nursing profession. Although they both married neither of them had children. Their nursing careers took them down to New South Wales where they lived for the rest of their lives, Edith in Sydney and Elizabeth in Goulburn. Grandfather remained on the farm with Uncle Arthur until his death in 1928.

On one of my visits to Aunt Edith she told me of a disturbing episode relating to Uncle Arthur when he was 20 years of age. To supplement the income from the farm he used to help out a local teamster, as and when he required an assistant to drive one of his oxen wagon teams. On this particular occasion the boss drove the front wagon with his six oxen and Uncle followed with his team. Aunt wasn't quite sure of the content of the cargo, but it was to be delivered to a large cattle station, somewhere in the outback. On the second day of their eight-day return journey back home his boss dropped down dead whilst harnessing his team for the day's work.

Uncle was faced with rather a tense situation. His first thought was to bury the corpse, but he realised that it might be a little embarrassing to arrive back in town without his boss, and have to explain his absence. Having made up his mind he loaded the body onto one of the wagons, hitched one team behind the other and drove both teams for the remainder of the journey back to base. Seemingly, he was praised by the local constabulary on his return for having the presence of mind to bring the body back with him and not to bury it.

As a young man William, the younger son, set off on his travels to explore the vast country, but after a few letters back home he was never heard of again, much to the grief of his family.

In 1972 our eldest daughter, Rosemary, also visited Australia. She took a few weeks off from a working year in New Zealand, having completed a BSc Degree in Agriculture at Wye. She made contact with my cousin Sid, a son of my late Uncle Arthur, and stayed with his family on their farm near Bowen on the Queensland coast. She was quite amazed to learn that she had so many relatives in Australia, all descendants of Uncle Arthur.

*

Now to get back to my dismal service in the Royal Navy. The news of the Japanese surrender early in August 1945 was greeted with what I would call mass hysteria in Sydney. In our camp on the race course in Liverpool great preparations were made for a mammoth bonfire which was to be torched at midnight.

At 5.00pm on that night the commander of the camp announced that he had arranged for a special train to run from Liverpool down to Sydney Pitt Street station to enable us join in the Victory celebrations that were already taking place. The lighting of the bonfire was to be postponed until our return to camp at a much later time. The scene that greeted us downtown was one of utter chaos; throngs of people were dancing and singing with much gusto every wartime song that had ever been written. No stops were pulled, with *Waltzing Matilda* being exploited to its full potential for patriotism. Pitt Street, which had the largest concentration of revellers, was littered ankle-deep with paper and books that had been thrown out of the high-rise office blocks which bounded this main street of Sydney.

People of all ages were engaged in this merriment with the fair sex being in the majority, and most of the males not being too backward in accepting the hugs and kisses being so freely expressed!

Our train was due to take us back to Liverpool at 2.00am; most of us caught it, with the rest having to make their own way back to camp the following morning. On our return we found that our bonfire was down to its last embers, having been started by the few men who had chosen not to join in the city celebrations.

A couple of days after the surrender of Japan volunteers were being asked to take part in either the occupation of Tokyo or Hong Kong. I chose the latter and 24 hours later I was aboard HMS Vindex en route to the colony. The Vindex was an aircraft carrier which had started its life as a banana boat, plying between the West Indies and Liverpool. Several of these same boats had been brought into use at different periods of the War and had given good service in various roles.

We arrived in Hong Kong on 20th August to find a large part of the British Pacific fleet already there, with the flagship HMS Anson very much in evidence. The Japanese garrison had surrendered very willingly and were all interned on the mainland at Kowloon, awaiting transport back to their homeland.

Along with several other men from all branches of the RN we took up billets in different parts of the dockyard area. For the whole five months that I was stationed in the Colony my billet was in the St. Francis Hotel, which was a very unkempt establishment, a few hundred yards from the dockyard gates. It had been occupied by Japanese troops since they captured the colony in 1941, and was in rather a filthy state. The Chinese boys who took control of it soon had it cleaned up into quite a respectable billet, and the food they cooked for us was superb, considering the sparse amount of raw material they had to work with. Their masterpiece of ingenuity was the way they made delicious chips from dehydrated potato flour - almost as good as King Edwards!

The Colony was in a very run-down condition after nearly four years of enemy occupation and a lot of work was called for. The city of Victoria, together with the dock area, had been severely damaged with American precision-bombing. It was some weeks before the power stations were able to transmit any electric power to the grid.

Most of the tram lines were intact, and three old tram cars appeared from nowhere, with power supplied from a flotilla of submarines tied up in the dockyard. A skeleton tramcar service was started. Now the Chinese inhabitants of Hong Kong, having been denied the pleasure of this form of transport for the whole time of the Japanese occupation, lost no time in making up for this hardship. The sight of these old trams creeping along at snail speed, grossly overloaded with people of all ages, enjoying free rides by courtesy of the British Government, is a sight that I will always remember. The cars were packed full and from each window were hanging at least four other travellers, with small children clutching onto the shoulders of the ones above.

There were two dry docks in the dockyard, but there was no coal to fuel the boilers to supply steam to the pumps in order to drain the docks and carry out urgent repairs to various ships. By some unknown piece of good fortune a cargo ship laden with cord wood was diverted into the harbour, and discharged its full load onto the quayside close by the power station.

I was given the job of supervising the removal of this timber from the waterfront into the boiler room, a distance of about one hundred yards. My workforce consisted of 40 coolies, mostly boys from the age of 10 years up. They were a happy crowd to work with and they moved a vast number of logs in the matter of a few days. They worked in pairs, two boys sharing one bamboo pole about eight feet in length, with a rope sling suspended in the middle of it. This sling was bound round the log, and with one end of the pole on each of their shoulders, they would trot along and discharge the load at the entrance to the boiler room.

Some of these logs weighed up to 150lbs and the boys would struggle along quite happily with them, but some were just a few pounds and no way could they be persuaded to carry more than one of these at any time. At the end of the afternoon the boys would muster at the dockyard gates to collect their reward for the day's work. At this period of time the Colony was without any official currency, and most transactions were in kind until the Hong Kong dollar got back into circulation. Just inside the dockyard gates was a large heap of brown rice, and it was from this heap that all the coolies got their payment at the end of each day. The Master at Arms, along with other senior ratings, carried out the distribution of this rice; each boy received one Catty of grain (the equivalent of 1⅓lbs). I believe the senior coolies were entitled to more generous portions.

On emerging from the dockyard gates the bearers of rice were quickly surrounded by the local community, willing to barter all types of commodities just for a small amount of their staple diet.

This situation didn't last for many weeks and once the currency was back in circulation things soon became normal. By mid-September the shops were overflowing with goods and the shopkeepers had a heyday selling their wares to the many thousands of British and Allied servicemen keen to take home souvenirs from this exotic colony. Where all these treasures had been hidden throughout the Japanese occupation was quite a mystery. In just a few weeks silk, jade, ivory, ebony carvings and many other oriental goods were on sale in the shops.

I was always a bit on the mean side when it came to parting with my money but I did push the boat out a little and buy a few small keepsakes. Over 60 years later, I am quite proud of this small collection that I hope will remain in the family.

After a couple of weeks looking after the discharge of logs to the boiler rooms, I was disappointed to find the engineers had converted both of the boilers to oil burners and the load of wood wasn't needed after all. What happened to this great stack of wood I never did find out, as by now I had been detailed off to a fresh job. I was put in charge of a small group of Chinese refrigeration engineers whose work was to carry out service and repair work at various military and government establishments on the island. My knowledge of refrigeration was nil, but that was of no consequence as my number one boy, by the name of Lam-Yik-Man, was a brilliant engineer who had served his apprenticeship with the Kelvinator Refrigeration company in his early days, and had served as an engineer with the American army for several years.

The rest of my time in Hong Kong was spent working happily with Lam-Yik-Man and his two mates (whose names I can't remember). He was a great talker and told me lots of stories about his boyhood and his time in the army, but his main joy was seeing the Royal naval ships back in Hong Kong harbour. He had a wife and two young sons and I had the pleasure of being invited to join them to share Sunday breakfast on several occasions.

A lot of our work consisted of the maintenance of the various refrigeration units in the Queen Mary Hospital which was situated high up on the Peak which dominated the centre of the island. One morning we were summoned to attend a defect at the mortuary. Before we could commence work seven bodies, all wrapped in white shrouds, had to be removed from the shelves.

The Christmas of 1945 is one that still stands out clearly in my memory. In the St. Francis Hotel, where about 50 naval personnel were billeted, was a certain Sick Berth Attendant (SBA) by the name of Roland. This man had spent many years as a globe trotter, working in various occupations on four different continents, but by the end of 1940 he was employed in a hospital in Tokyo and decided that he should get home to England.

After a prolonged voyage back home he joined the Royal Navy as an SBA. On this particular Christmas morning Rolly managed, by fair means or foul, to acquire a Jeep for our private use for the whole day. After the morning church parade and service, six of us set out in this Jeep, following the road around the island, through the village of Aberdeen and on to Repulse Bay where we stopped for a quick dip in the chilly water. The fact that we didn't have one pair of swimming trunks between us was of no great embarrassment as we were well out-of-sight of any of the local maidens! We then passed by the Stanley Internment Camp which was now free of all the British subjects who had spent the whole of the Japanese occupation years within its walls.

Further on round the island we came across a very attractive-looking sandy beach and decided to drive onto it. After a couple of turns around it, lots of the children from the adjoining village started to appear, and in a very short while we found ourselves giving these kids joy rides up and down the beach. With just the driver and one assistant, about eight kids at a time piled onto the Jeep and, with much merriment, would do a couple of turns before disembarking. On would get the next load, ready for their bit of excitement. As the afternoon wore on the crowd of joy riders had swelled to about 40.

After a couple of hours of this entertainment we were delighted when the local schoolmaster came out to join us and invited us all to go back to the schoolhouse and share tea with him and his wife. This was a most enjoyable little party, sitting on the flat roof of this schoolhouse, drinking milk and sugarless tea out of traditional Chinese teacups, with rather exotic biscuits to accompany it. At the end of the tea drinking, we were delighted to be asked if we would like to hear the children sing some of their native songs. These they sang with great gusto, not that we could understand their language, but the enthusiasm with which they sang made up for our lack of the Cantonese dialect. When the time came for us to depart, the schoolmaster had all the children line up in the playground and each one give us a very impressive bow as we walked past them. I doubt if the Admiral of the Fleet could have aroused more enthusiasm.

Another memorable occasion occurred one time when I met up with a mate, Paddy Kelly, who was serving on the battleship, HMS Anson. I'd seen him a few times since arriving in the colony and, at one of our meetings at the Fleet Club, he told me of an Australian (a member of the Hong Kong Police, interned by the Japanese throughout the War years) who had asked him if he knew anything about domestic refrigerators. The flat where he lived was in a sad state when he returned to it after his release from the POW camp in Repulse Bay. With the aid of his Chinese mistress he had renovated the flat into a suitable condition to take up residence, except that the refrigerator was not working. Paddy told him that he had a mate (me) working with a party of refrigeration engineers in the dockyard and he was sure that it could be fixed.

Arrangements were made and Paddy and I met the policeman at the dockyard gates. He drove us to his flat, showed us the refrigerator and said, "When you have completed the job you will find a couple of bottles on my desk which I hope will be empty on my return. I will not be able to drive you back to the dockyard, as duty calls, but have left instructions with my housekeeper to call for a couple of rickshaws when you are ready to leave."

I think we completed the job satisfactorily, but the two bottles that were left as our reward were the cause of two very sore heads for a couple of days. I have a vivid memory of my rickshaw drawing up at the St. Francis Hotel and the Chinese boy being very reluctant for me to leave the rickshaw until I had paid my fare which I believe was two HK dollars. The following morning I was woken up by one of my room mates with the words, "Here you are, Stan, a cup of tea, of which you must be in full need".

Whilst drinking that cup of tea I heard the full account of my arrival at the door of the St. Francis the previous evening. With me being well out in the land of nod the rickshaw boy had gone through my pockets in search of some money, but found them completely blank. All he found was my station card with my accommodation address on it. The CPO in charge paid the fare and got rid of the boy who, in turn, must have been quite relieved to be shot of me.

The next time that I met up with Paddy he told me that he too had a sore head to contend with, but at least he had money in his pocket to pay the rickshaw boy. He also remembered that the contents of those two bottles consisted of whisky in the one and gin in the other. Little wonder that we both got such sore heads, with neither of us being used to such expensive liquor.

*

Early in January 1946 I was informed that my demob number would shortly be coming up so to be prepared to be drafted back to the UK. On the fifth of that month I joined HMS Apollo en route back to Sydney.

The Apollo was a mine-laying cruiser and had been built specifically for laying mines during the hours of darkness. She was capable of speeds up to 46 knots and most of her time had been spent speeding out of the port of Harwich and racing across the North Sea, laying her mines in the Hook of Holland, and back in Harwich before the break of day.

Accommodation for the crew was rather on the limited side and us 10 ratings who were thrust on them just to take passage to Sydney, stretched it to the limit. After a discussion with the officer of the watch we were given permission to live down in the bilge of the ship where the mines were mostly stored.

The voyage to Australia was uneventful, other than a typhoon which struck us during our passage through the Celebes Sea. We 10 passengers were confined to the depths of the ship for the 36 hours that it took the typhoon to blow itself out.

On disembarking at Sydney on 11th January we were taken to the new naval camp that had been built at Liverpool. I was able to visit my aunt and uncle on several occasions before my departure back to the UK. They were quite sad at our final farewell, having had a family reunion after all these years. I remember promising them that I would make a return visit to Australia and meet the rest of the Lane family who were mostly living in Queensland. Sadly, as yet I have not fulfilled that promise, but am still hoping to make the effort. Several of the Lanes have since been over here and we have had the pleasure of showing them parts of our country, including Upton Court Farm in the parish of Leysters, Herefordshire, which the Lane family had farmed from 1705 until their departure to Australia in 1887.

On 21st January 1946 I joined HMS Victorious en route to the UK. This ship was one of our largest aircraft carriers and had been in action in various theatres of the War at sea, including the final months of the Japanese campaign.

All of her aircraft had been left in Sydney, thus enabling her to accommodate the 1,500 passengers who were taking passage back to the UK to be demobbed. The ship's crew of 1,000 men remained in their own quarters. The empty hangars and workshops provided the rather cramped sleeping quarters for all of these extra folk. 150 nurses and Wrens who were taking passage were allotted the most private of the available space. The men were left to sleep wherever they could find a space to put their collapsible beds. I, along with three mates, looked around for a place to doss and with a bit of good luck found one of the four-inch gun turrets unoccupied, and in this rather cramped space we took up residence for the 38 days that it took us to reach the UK.

Unlike most of the people we four didn't suffer from complete boredom. From amongst my kit I fished out a pack of playing cards and we started playing Solo Whist - on average for 12 hours a day for the whole time that we spent on the Victorious. Gambling with cash was strictly forbidden on HMS ships, but with pencil and paper, and a bit of honest bookkeeping, this problem was overcome in private. The stakes were very low risk. To anyone who may not be familiar with pre-decimal currency, the call of Solo was worth one penny, Mizare twopence, Abundance threepence, Mizare of Aire fourpence, and the top call of all, Abundance Declare five pence. At the final countdown on the day before we disembarked at Plymouth, the highest gain by one of the team was nine shillings. My score was minus two shillings and eight pence, not a big price to pay for a voyage halfway around the world.

Our first port of call was at Fremantle. The captain of HMS Victorious must to this day regret ever giving four hours' shore leave to all passengers and crew, other than the duty watch.

We disembarked at Fremantle docks at midday with strict instructions to be back on board by 1600 hours prompt! I, along with a couple of hundred other men, complied with this order and made sure we were back in good time. In 1946 Fremantle had little to interest such a great influx of passengers and crew off a large aircraft carrier, other than an abundance of bars. At that time Australian bars had to close at 6.00pm: aware of this bit of knowledge, our crowd inflicted great pressure on the barmen to drink them all dry by closing time. This target was achieved well within the limit!

By this time the officers on duty were getting a little anxious as to when the rest of the crowd would make it back to the ship. Urgent appeals were made to the Australian military forces to round up these wayward revellers and escort them back. Eventually army trucks began to arrive at the dockside, discharge these rather boisterous passengers and then make their way back downtown to collect another load. It was nearly 7.00pm when the last convoy of trucks discharged the final consignment!

The Victorious finally sailed at 10.00pm, three hours later than scheduled. Quite a few of the over-noisy revellers were put into close confinement for the night, and were released the following morning with a few sore heads between them. After a couple of days at sea and a final role call had been made, it turned out that 21 passengers had been left behind in Fremantle and six non-members of the Victorious had managed to make their way on board, with the idea of returning to the UK prematurely. These men were dropped off at Singapore, our next port of call. What happened to the 21 who were left behind, I never found out.

As a result of this rather disastrous afternoon's shore leave in Fremantle, the Captain, by way of punishment, banned all shore leave until our arrival back in the UK. The one exception to this ban was a concession in favour of all the female members who were on board. Whilst being tied up alongside this long wharf in Singapore all these ladies, smartly dressed in their uniforms, disembarked and were mustered into an impressive-looking body of military splendour. I think the whole idea of this exercise was to give these ladies a chance to stretch their limbs and also to impress the local dock yard workers! After marching up and down the dockside a few times, the skies began to look a little suspect and, as they were doing their about-turn at the further end of the dockside, the heavens opened and down came one of the most severe rain storms that I have ever seen.

In the five minutes it took this party to make the final march back to the ship they got well and truly soaked to the skin, and instead of the very smart party that set out, they resembled a large group of drowned rats. During the final hundred yards of their march the men on board broke into a very noisy bout of cheering which got louder as the ladies crossed the gangway.

The remainder of the passage home was uneventful, calling at Colombo, Aden, Port Said and Gibraltar, all without being allowed any shore leave as a result of the episode at Fremantle. We arrived at Plymouth on 4th March. As I was a Portsmouth rating, along with several others, we were sent by rail to RNB Portsmouth to await our demob, which in my case came on 26 May 1946.

After finally being signed off I was issued with a rail ticket back home and a voucher to take along to the Southdown Bus Station at

Cosham and claim my demob kit. This consisted of a tweed suit, a shirt, a pair of shoes and socks, and a hat of my choice - a Trilby or a flat cap. The latter was happily received as I was by now looking forward to wearing my favourite headgear. I never did wear the suit, as my brother Arthur took rather a liking to it and offered to buy it. I gladly accepted the £5 that he offered me.

In addition to the clothes that we were issued, we were allowed to keep our uniforms, plus our hammock and blanket, both of which are still in our household today, nearly 60 years on. Both of our daughters and our four grandchildren have spent a few happy hours swinging in the hammock suspended between the apple trees in the garden, which says a lot for the superior quality of material used by the RN.

On my arrival home I was at a bit of a loose end, like thousands of other returning service men, not being too sure of what lay in store. Four years and six months had passed since I joined the Royal Navy, with the expectation of serving my country in a far more active role than I was destined to achieve. I suppose that I should think myself lucky that I came out of the war unscathed.

Left: in Trafalgar Square, c.1943. Mary (centre), Jennie (right) and friend

Below: Uncle Arthur, Aunts Edith and Elizabeth, Stan's father's siblings, in Australia

Looking into mainland China from Kowloon

Lam-Yik-Man, a fellow
Engineer in Hong Kong

Stan, on the balcony of the
St. Francis Hotel, Hong Kong

WRENS SAY FAREWELL TO SYDNEY AS CARRIER SAILS

When H.M.S. Victorious sailed from Sydney Harbour late yesterday afternoon, bound for England, the ship's complement were drawn up in divisions and the Wrens lined the forward flight deck.

8. Return To The Land

Mr Reg Evans, with whom I had worked for the four and a half years after leaving school until joining the RN, had now sold his milk round, and moved to a larger farm. He offered me my old job back, but I decided that I would look further afield. My brother Syd, who had taken over the tenancy of Magnolia Farm in 1942, was ill at this time and his wife Ann was having a hard time looking after the farm and two small sons, Tony and Victor. I offered to go and help them out, and that is where I spent the summer of 1946. Magnolia Farm was one of a group of seven small farms all within close proximity of each other in the hamlet of Cannon Bridge, which lies alongside the River Wye, six miles north of Hereford.

This group of farms were farmed by a very close knit community, each one of them taking great pride in the appearance of their farms and livestock. Not much went amiss without it being observed by one or other of the neighbours and put to rights. At that time only two of them possessed a tractor, the rest relying on horse power to do the work of mowing, rolling, ploughing, carting and all the other tasks.

Five of these farms had dairy herds ranging in size from 12 to 20 cows, with Syd's being one of the larger ones. In those days the most popular breed was the Dairy Shorthorn, with the British Friesian just beginning to make its appearance. Most of these farms had by then installed milking machines which made life a little easier for them. Four of the farms shared a common green road down to the pastures, and this was the situation that caused an occasional hiccup with the passage of cows to and from milking, but nothing that a few friendly words couldn't put right.

Amongst these neighbours was one, Stan Morgan, a confirmed bachelor, who was a traditional, old-type countryman. He was a great teller of tales, most of them true, but after a few beers he was quite capable of stretching his imagination, much to the amusement of his listeners. One day in mid-June he asked my brother if he could borrow me for a few hours to help shear his sheep that evening. Syd readily agreed but said to him, "Just go a bit easy on the cider!" Now whether he didn't hear this bit of advice, or chose to ignore it, I never knew.

His flock consisted of 17 Crossbred ewes and my task was to turn the handle on the shearing machine as he performed the clipping. On the first one being finished in good time Stan suggested we should celebrate with a small tot of cider. Now, not paying too much heed to Syd's warning, I readily agreed to join him, thinking that maybe I would be offered another one on completion of the job. How wrong I was, as at the completion of each ewe he insisted that we partake in another small tot.

These tots were made out of the horns of cattle, hollowed out to make drinking vessels, and were in common use in the Welsh border counties. They would be placed at the side, or on top of the barrel, and to my recollection never did get washed. The tots contained about a quarter of a pint, and after drinking the health of each sheep as she had her fleece removed, I thought that the party was over. But no, Stan suggested that he harness Blossom, his black mare, hitch her to the spring cart and take a trip to The Red Lion, the pub in the village of Madley, a distance of two miles from the farm.

Stan, not being a regular attendant at this pub, was greeted by several of his old friends, all eager to drink his health. Whilst seeing off a few pints, stories began to flow to the enjoyment of all the people in the bar. Some time during the merriment he had accepted the offer of a black cat, and also had arranged to collect it on our way home. At closing time we collected Blossom who had been tied up in the yard adjoining the pub and set off. By now it was pitch dark and we had no lights on the trap for our homeward trip. The owner of the cat lived in a cottage about halfway on our journey and he had arranged to meet us by the roadside, but alas, when we arrived at this place he wasn't there. Stan suggested that he went to seek him out if I would stay and look after Blossom. Now why it took him so long to walk no more than 50 yards, I never did know, but rather suspect that they had to drink to the health of the cat in its new home, and the fact that Stan was relieving him of one of his surplus cats! After nearly an hour he came back to the horse and trap and handed the cat to me to hold. We set off back to the farm with me thinking that it might slip free, but I was determined not to let that happen as I didn't fancy looking for a black cat in complete darkness. Eventually we got home about midnight and put the cat in his back kitchen for safety. Stan had an elderly, very austere housekeeper who tried hard to keep him in order, and on coming downstairs the next morning she was aghast to find a cat sitting on the hearth in the kitchen. She didn't want a cat in the house, and this she made clear to him when he came into his breakfast. She won the day and Stan had to take the cat back to its owner, with what excuse I never knew.

After three months helping my brother during his illness, the time had come for me to find a permanent job and I went along to the Ministry of Agriculture, Fisheries and Food (MAFF) office in Worcester and made inquiries about getting a permanent job in the locality. I was told that a good job was becoming available shortly and they would let me know as soon as they were certain about it. In the meantime they were looking for help on a farm just a few miles out of the city.

Whilst staying with my sister Mary, I spent two weeks working on this farm. The owner had been compelled by the War Ag. to plough up 150 acres of his best meadowland to grow cereals and potatoes. This land was alongside the River Severn and was of highly fertile, alluvial soil. It was subject to flooding and in August 1946, when the wheat had been cut and stooked and the potatoes were still in the ground, extremely heavy rain caused severe flooding in the Severn Valley.

Practically all of this land was flooded and, as the water receded, it took the stooks of wheat with it. Most of it was washed down the river and flowed towards Severn Stoke and beyond. Quite a lot finished up in the willow trees that lined the river bank. The recovery of these wheat sheaves was the task of the working gang that I joined. The sheaves were all grown together and it was quite a job pulling them apart, throwing them up on the river bank and spreading them out to dry. I never knew the final fate of these practically worthless sheaves.

That evening, when I got back to my sister's, a letter was waiting for me from Les Powell, offering me a job at Parkmoor Farm, Torton, a village a couple of miles out of Kidderminster. The next day I went over to see him and was taken on immediately, with the comment: "If you are Arthur Lane's brother and you are only half as reliable as him you can start here next Monday."

Parkmoor Farm was 500 acres of an easy-working, sandy loam soil which needed a lot of feeding, but responded well to the right treatment. Apart from a small area of grass it all came under cultivation, with the main crops being sugar beet, potatoes, Brussels sprouts and various varieties of broccoli and cabbage. Other crops on smaller acreage included beetroot, strawberries, runner beans and radishes. There was also several acres used for the production of flowers that were now allowed to be grown again, after several years of wartime restriction. The other crop that was grown was dredge corn (a mixture of spring wheat, barley and oats). This crop was being grown solely for feeding the poultry unit. If cereals were grown straight they couldn't be retained for use on the farm, but were compulsorily purchased by the MAFF, but dredge corn could be used only on the farm where it was produced. About 100 acres of this crop was grown to help feed the poultry unit that was being extended to accommodate several thousand laying hens, all in battery cages.

During the three and a half years that I worked on this farm I partook in a variety of tasks, with tractor driving being one of the most frequent. The winter of 1947 turned out to be one of the most severe of the 20th century. Heavy snow fell in early January, accompanied by very severe frosts, and more snowstorms followed. The thaw didn't come until early April which meant that the planting of spring crops was severely disrupted. The job that I helped with during the whole of January and most of February is one that I will never forget. The farm staff, which consisted of six men and some German POWs who lived in one of the farm cottages, were set to work harvesting 36 acres of Savoy cabbages. The field where they were grown was completely exposed to the north wind, which didn't fail to make itself known all day and every day. These cabbages were completely covered with several inches of snow and frozen solid. They were only distinguishable by the lumps of snow that covered the field, row upon row of them, about 17,000 per acre. Harvesting involved three men, each with the aid of a spade, to follow a row of these completely invisible cabbages, make a sharp blow under the lumps of snow to cut the short stalks. Following this operation the rest of the team, with the aid of forks, placed them into a cabbage mat which was woven out of coarse hemp string. Each mat, when full under normal conditions, would weigh about 40lbs, but in this case it was about 15lbs of cabbage and 25lbs of frozen snow. The mats were lifted onto tractors and trailers, taken down to the farm and carefully loaded onto the farm lorry, ready to be taken to the wholesale market in Birmingham the following morning.

From the farm there was a steep hill up to the main road and this called for a little extra traction with the road being so ice-bound. Power was given by two of us getting up at 4.30am each morning, hitching two tractors onto the lorry and pulling it up to the main road where it would set off for the early market. In those years immediately after the War all food was scarce and these cabbages found a ready sale.

I do not know what the housewives and restaurateurs thought of paying so dearly for frozen lumps of snow with a cabbage hiding in the centre. Each day during this monotonous job, at 9.00am, 11.00am and at 2.30pm, the boss turned up with a gallon jug of hot Bovril and, my goodness, weren't we all thankful for it.

Among the farm staff we had a couple of pipe smokers; one of them was rather a short exSergeant from the Army who thought he would make a career in farming but soon gave up the idea. The other one was a tall, rather gaunt, lifetime farm worker named Syd. Syd was well known for being rather light-fingered. One day, the Sergeant's tobacco, pipe and pouch went missing, much to his dismay. After a couple of days searching for them without success, he gave up hope of finding them and went up to the village to buy a replacement. A few days later a gang of us were engaged in cutting cauliflower when all of a sudden the Sergeant gave a leap forward, snatched his lost pipe out of Syd's mouth and gave him a most severe lecture on dishonesty and what might happen to him if he was caught repeating the operation. Now after about 10 minutes in deep thought Syd, being a little bit slow, put his hand in his jacket pocket, strolled over to where the sergeant had started working again, pulled his hand out of his pocket and said, quite innocently, "You may as well have the bloody pouch to go with it." At the time this was quite amusing to the other members of the working gang.

One day Syd had occasion to visit the local dentist as he was suffering with severe toothache. After extracting the tooth, the dentist went to the back of the surgery to get some dressing and, during his absence, Syd seized the opportunity to remove some surgical instruments from the table and place them in his pocket. A few days later, as I was passing the door of his cottage, Syd called me in and asked me to explain to what use he could put these instruments. After telling him that they would be of limited use to him, I suggested that he took them back to the surgery and tell the dentist that he had taken them whilst still under the influence of the local anaesthetic.

"Not bloody likely!" was Syd's reply. "He charged me half a crown to pull out my tooth, so I think I am well entitled to something for my money."

Another memory of Syd was one day sometime in late November, when he had been carting potatoes from a 20-acre field. A thick fog had persisted all day and the boss told us to knock off early whilst there was still a bit of light to get back to the farmyard, which was a good mile away across a busy road. A good hour after we had got back to the farm, Syd had failed to turn up, so two of us set off to walk the road and search for him. Alas, we didn't find him until we got back to the field where we had left him. There, after a little while, we heard the old Fordson tractor coming up the field and there was Syd sitting on the seat, smoking his pipe and looking out for the gateway, which he must have passed several times on his travels. In those days we didn't enjoy the luxury of lights on tractors, so we had to leave it in the field and leg it back to the farm, as by now it was completely dark and unsafe to take it on the road.

In the year 1948 I was given the job of planting 115 acres of potatoes, carrying out all the inter-row cultivation required and, at the end of July, harvesting the crop. The planting was completed by mid-April at an average daily output of eight acres. A new three-row planter had been purchased that season. This became the envy of the neighbouring farmers, with its superior speed of planting as opposed to the traditional hand planting method. I was assisted by three German POWs, who were excellent workers and rather keen to prove themselves worthy members of the Master Race!

Unlike today's chemical weed control, we had to carry out a rigid program of cultivation to ensure a clean crop of potatoes at harvest time. As soon as the weeds germinated, I went through them with a tractor and three-row cultivator and smothered them. This operation was repeated each time the weeds made a fresh germination, which amounted to three times that season. The final operation was earthing them up with a three-row mould plough, which apart from making sure that the potatoes were well covered, smothered the surviving weeds.

Each morning when harvesting started, I used to raise two rows of potatoes with an elevator digger, ready for the pickers to start work on their arrival at the field. I would collect the pickers, all ladies from the town of Stourport-on-Severn, in the farm lorry and return them at the end of the working day. Our target was to clear four acres daily and this was achieved on most days, with the picking gang getting paid a bonus for any area picked above the target.

The total gang of pickers amounted to 16. One of them, Mrs Barraclough, was the life and soul of the party. During the lunch break they would sit on the hedge bank, eating their sandwiches, whilst Mrs Barraclough entertained them with episodes from her school days, teenage years and marriage, and any problems that she seemed to have encountered. She also kept them in stitches, relating the dubious activities of some of the inhabitants of the area where she lived. On the third morning that I picked them up in the farm lorry, she was quite distressed. Her pet goat, Lop Ears, was missing her company during working hours and each evening had failed to give any milk. We all commiserated with her and suggested that after a few more days Lop Ears would get used to her daily absence. This didn't happen and a few mornings later, when stopping to collect her, there she was waiting at her garden gate with Lop Ears on a lead, asking if she could bring the animal with her to work.

I said, "Yes, I'm sure the boss will not mind if I tell him that your goat is suffering from severe depression due to your absence each day."

She answered, "It's not depression on the goat's part, it's one of my lousy neighbours that's causing the trouble. Yesterday, when we all knocked off work a bit early, I arrived home to find Lop Ears tied up to the gate, being milked out into a large enamel jug." The mystery of the daily lack of milk was solved. She had been so livid with this mean act, that she had rushed over to the said neighbour, snatched the jug of milk off her and poured the contents down her neck. She then spent a good five minutes calling her all the names she could muster and finally expressed grave doubts about her parentage. Each morning after this, Lop Ears was lifted onto the lorry and, after a few days, she jumped up of her own accord. On arrival in the field she was tied up in the hedgerow. She became a great favourite with all the ladies and each lunchtime would get lots of titbits, her favourite snack being to chew a little bit off any garment that she could reach. Goats are a bit like that.

All the potatoes were clamped in the field and covered with straw and a good covering of soil to protect them from the frost. This was quite a time-consuming job, with well over 1,000 tons to cover that season. They were all sold through Birmingham market, starting in October and finishing by the end of February.

I used to drive one of the two lorries that belonged to the farm. Each of us would take a six-ton load and some days managed three loads, especially if we got a 5.00am start.

One afternoon on my return trip I got flagged down by a large crowd of people who were standing at the entrance to the Austin motor works at Longbridge. A bus strike had been called at midday and they pleaded with me to give them a lift home as most of them lived in the villages of Rubery and Marlbrook. As I would be passing through both of these places I readily agreed to help them. Little did I realise that over 40 of them would climb on the back of the lorry and three more in the cab. I dropped the last of my guests at Marlbrook, a good six-mile journey from the Austin works.

They were very appreciative of my kindness and handed me a biscuit tin, half full with coins of all sorts. One of the ladies had made the collection en route. When I got home and counted these coins I found that my rewards amounted to more than a week's wage.

During the summer of 1948 came the most important milestone in my life. On 19th June Mary and I got married at St. Mark's Church, Dalston, East London. I first got to know Mary when she came as a Land Girl to work beside me and my brother Arthur at the Valley Farm, Fockbury, Worcestershire, in December 1939. At that time I was just a boy of 16 and it took me the best part of nine years to await meeting her at the altar, but it was time very well spent. Now, many years on, I am still very proud of her, and so thankful to her for looking after me so well all these years.

We spent our week-long honeymoon at St. Catherine's, a small hamlet on the shore of Loch Fyne. Having no transport of our own, we had to make use of the local bus services to get around to do any sightseeing. There was a motor launch which made a couple of trips each day to Inverary across the other side of the Loch.

In the small hotel where we stayed we had to share a table with a retired Rear Admiral, and his rather timid wife. His method of communication with her was through a variety of grunts with which she seemed to be very familiar, and after two sharp grunts, followed by a softer one, she would pass him the sugar or whatever item he would point his finger at. On meeting Mary and I each morning we were greeted with two quite heavy grunts, which we took to mean "Good Morning", and we replied in the more traditional form of address. Looking back all those years ago that week we spent in his company is quite amusing, but at that time it was rather an embarrassment.

The farm cottage that we were allotted was in the tiny village of Shenstone, a couple of miles away from the farm. It was semi-detached and built about the turn of the century. Like a lot of farm cottages of that time it was rather short of some of the amenities which are a must today. Electricity had been laid on, but our water supply came from a well in the garden, from which we hand-pumped it into buckets for use in the house. The toilet was just a bucket in a shed near the back door, with the contents having to be buried in the large garden. The only other outdoor building was a pig sty, a usual addition to farm cottages in that part of the country.

The sty was soon occupied by two saddle-back weaner pigs, one for ourselves and one for my brother Arthur. Wartime rationing of animal feed stuffs still prevailed at that time, but all home keepers of pigs were allocated a monthly allowance of feed, to be supplemented with household scraps, which in our case didn't amount to a great deal. I used to get the odd bag of ground corn off the boss which was a great help to get these pigs up to the right weight. When they had grown to about 15 score they were taken to Marsh & Baxter's bacon factory and we got the cured hams and flitches back after a couple of weeks.

The present-day supporters of the anti-hunt movement are very keen to point out the fact that foxes only kill to eat their prey. How wrong they are. Early one morning in the summer of 1949 I happened to look out of our bedroom window and just across the field there were several hundred free-range pullets.

A fox was quietly going about his work, killing these birds without disturbing the rest of the poultry flock. With one clean bite at the top of the neck these pullets just dropped dead. After getting partly dressed in double-quick time, Mary and I rushed over to the part of the field where this massacre was being carried out. The fox ignored my shouting, but with a more vigorous screech from Mary he got the message and ran off. After 100 yards he had the cheek to stop and look back in anger at being disturbed at his little game. He had killed 34 of these birds and not eaten one of them, what a waste.

During the years since then, being more involved with sheep, I have seen many lambs that have been killed by a fox, but only partly eaten. There are occasions when a lamb has been found dead and the fox has been blamed for its death when it could well have died on its own.

During my time at Parkmoor Farm I got involved in a few tasks of an unusual kind. One that stands out clearly was the ploughing in of nine acres of blood-red wallflowers. These had been planted with the idea of them coming onto the market just before Easter, but unfortunately they were still in bud at that time and when they came into full flower 10 days later they had missed the lucrative sales. After the first load was returned to the farm as being unsaleable I was told to plough the lot of them in. It was a depressing sight to see all these beautiful, red wallflowers disappear under the plough and out of sight.

The hungry soil on this farm required as much humus as it was possible to come by. An important quantity came in the form of wool shoddy from the blanket factory in the lovely old town of Witney in Oxfordshire. During the War this factory was unable to get supplies of wool, which came mostly from Australia and South America. When the shipping became available to transport this product once again, vast quantities were imported to make up the backlog of five long years without supplies. As a result, the blankets were in great demand and the factory worked almost 24 hours a day to supply these needs.

Les Powell, who was always looking ahead, made a contract to take all this shoddy away and keep the factory clear. This involved going down with two lorries once a month to Witney, a distance of about 60 miles. With the help of two POWs we would fork by hand as much as we could possibly stack on the lorries. In case you are wondering what shoddy is, it is the residue from the cleaning and carding of the fleeces of wool. Apart from its fertility value, it would remain as a great soil conditioner for several years.

In those days we didn't enjoy the pleasure of mechanical muck spreaders, it all had to be spread by hand fork, which if the weather was kind was quite a pleasant job.

The boss also made a contract with a glue-extraction factory in Dudley, an industrial town in the Black Country. The glue was extracted from the gut and skins of cattle and our job was to clear away all the leftovers from this operation. This was a most unpleasant job; you may well imagine what this offal would smell like after being in a clamp, sometimes for several weeks. One particular hot summer's day, having loaded the two lorries and started our drive back to the farm, we pulled into a transport cafe to get a quick cup of tea. Before we even got out of the cab the proprietor, who must have smelled us before we pulled up, came tearing out and told us to get to hell out of it, as he could well do without our stinking custom. When this obnoxious material was spread on the land all the rooks from miles around seemed to descend on the field and make a meal of it before it was ploughed in.

The family at Jennie's wedding to Ernie Goodman in November, 1948. From right: Frank, Mary, Stan, Jennie, Syd, Edith and Arthur

9. Pastures New

In the spring of 1950, after a lot of discussion, Mary and I decided that we would move down to Kent or Sussex and set about looking for a farm, either to rent or maybe buy. We thought it would be good to move nearer to Mary's parents, who at that time were still living in London, but had a small bungalow close to the sea at Pett Level on the Sussex coast. It was to this place that we moved in July. We had just purchased our first motor vehicle so at last we were mobile, which was quite a step up from cycling. Mary's brother, Tom, had acquired this vehicle somewhere on his travels. It got christened 'The Beetle Box' owing to its rather austere conversion from a 1932 Morris Minor into a sort-of utility van, painted battleship grey. It cost £60 and gave us good service during the four years that we had it, and was sold for £25 when we acquired a Ford van complete with side windows!

Moving down to Pett and starting to look for a farm was rather unrewarding and, realising we had not enough capital to even think of buying one, we gave up for the time being. I got a temporary job with a local contractor, who ran two threshing machines for the Ministry of Agriculture with whom he had contracted to service an area of an eight-mile radius of Pett. The majority of the farms were quite small, only growing a small acreage of cereals, mostly on land which had been ploughed up from grassland soon after the outbreak of War. After a week working with one of these machines, I was put in charge of one and spent the next two months travelling to the various farms that needed our service. The length of time on each farm stretched from just half a day to four days.

Moving along some of the narrow lanes was a nightmare, with only a Fordson major tractor to pull the heavy threshing machine, which had steel wheels to run on. Mostly, the tractor brakes were sufficient to hold on the average hills, but on some of the steeper ones the rear wheels had to be tied with a chain that completely immobilised them. One particular hill that stands out in my mind is the one at Winchelsea that runs under the Strand Gate. I only had to descend it once which I found quite stressful and was glad to reach the bottom. On top of the week's wages, I received a bonus for the belt hours that were worked and was quite elated on being told that I was achieving more hours than were expected of me - which was also to the benefit of the contractor.

In our search for a farm to buy or rent - but with little hope of getting - Mary and I set off one day to look at three farms for which we had been sent the particulars. The first was Cold Blow Farm, Woodchurch, and there we met Stan Rogers who with his wife, Did, became lifelong friends of ours. He had been a tenant on the farm since 1941. The owner had now decided to sell it, and Stan rather wanted to buy it, hence some of my questions to him about the farm were answered rather uncomplimentary as to its viability.

The next farm that we visited was Little Bedgebury Farm in High Halden. We weren't over-impressed with what we saw and moved on to Little Omenden Farm, Biddenden. A commercial traveller was in the farmhouse in discussion with the owner, and waiting at the back door was an elderly gentleman.

After exchanging the time of day he said, "I don't seem to recognise your face, are you local?"

I replied that this was the first time that I had ever been in the area. I explained that I was looking for a farm to either buy or rent and it was proving rather difficult to find anything that suited my wants - and more particularly my pocket.

He responded: "That is interesting, maybe I can be of some help to you". After these few words of encouragement he was called into the farmhouse and I waited awhile until he came out, expecting to carry on the conversation. However, the owner of the farm, seeing me with the land agent's leaflet in my hand, called me indoors, and the elderly gentleman mounted his bicycle and rode off. We discussed the farm and had a quick look around some of the land and the farm buildings. However, the price being asked was well out of our range so we suffered another disappointment.

On the Saturday afternoon of that week we decided to try and renew our brief encounter with the elderly gentleman. Not knowing either his name or address we visited the Post Office in Biddenden. The postmaster was very helpful and, after some thought, was certain that the gentleman we were seeking lived at Randolphs, a large Elizabethan house on the edge of the village. A little while after we rang the front door bell, Mr Herbert Gordon Jones, for that was his name, immediately invited us into the sitting room. He introduced us to his wife as a pair of strangers to the area that he had met midweek whilst out on his bicycle collecting an overdue payment from one of his neighbours. Over tea and scones, and delicious quince jelly, he explained what his farm consisted of and the length of time he had been there. After a long discussion it was decided that we should come to see him the following Saturday by when he would be in the position to offer us something to our advantage.

The outcome of this next interview was the beginning of a very happy, 12-year period of our life. Mr Gordon Jones employed me as his personal assistant, a position that also held a financial interest. In addition to the basic farm wage, I would receive a 25% share in the annual farm profits, with me paying him 5% interest on a quarter of the capital that he had invested in the farm.

This arrangement, which was completely verbal, lasted the full 12 years that I was at Randolphs, and not once did we have any cause to query it. So, on 10th October 1950 we moved into Randolph Lodge Farm, remaining there until 1962. The farmhouse was quite extensive with six bedrooms and all the usual offices. We had to wait seven years until electricity was installed. There was a large garden with several fruit trees and four Kent cobnut trees which the grey squirrels treated as their very own source of food.

The farm consisted of 85 acres, with a further 120 acres at River Hall Farm, which was a couple of miles distant. The farm was a traditional mixed Weald farm with beef, sheep, and pigs, and some arable on which was grown wheat, oats, barley and, until 1954, flax. This latter crop had been grown widely during the War years, on contract to the flax-processing factory situated at Pluckley, until its closure that year. In those days, before the common use of herbicides, weeds were a big problem with growing flax.

In the harvest of 1951 the contractor arrived with a mechanical flax puller, but before the driver had gone a hundred yards round the field, he had found that the vast amount of cleavers present in the crop made it impossible for the machine to either pull the flax or to tie it up into sheaves. The whole crop had to be pulled and tied by hand, which was a most tedious job, and we were well pleased when the last of this seven-acre crop was completed.

In addition, 20 acres of apples and three acres of plums were grown. The apple trees had been planted in 1896 during the first year that Mr Gordon Jones had moved to the farm. Like a lot of orchards at that time many varieties were planted, with Randolph Lodge having 34, but they had been whittled down to just 14 when we moved there. The varieties were fairly evenly divided between desert and culinary: Bramleys and Newton Wonders made up most of the culinary area with Beauty of Bath, Worcester Permains, Cox Orange Pippins, Millers Seedling and Laxton Superb being the main desert varieties. With so many it was

112

difficult to find the optimum time for spraying, but a moderate success rate was achieved.

The sheep flock consisted of about 220 Romney ewes - or Kents as they were commonly known of in those days. Lambing was in mid-March with an average lambing percentage of 120. The lambs were all sold at the Tenterden Annual Fair which was held in the first week of September. It was at this Fair that Bill Deacon, the shepherd, and I were awarded one shilling each for presenting such a good show of lambs. This practice was carried out for all the years that I was at Randolphs. Inflation hadn't become an everyday utterance in those days. The value of these lambs was about £5 in 1951 and had only risen to close on £7 in 1962. Each autumn 30 to 40 ewe tegs were bought, to keep up the flock numbers to replace deaths and culls.

The beef cattle consisted of four Shorthorn suckler cows which would rear about four calves each during a lactation. Extra calves were bought in Ashford Market for this purpose. In those days Shorthorns were the most popular dairy breed in this area and we bought the surplus bull calves. The Sussex was the only beef bull used for crossing in those days. These Crossbred calves were worth a premium of about £2 over the red or roan Shorthorn calves, which at that time were worth in the region of about £3. These cattle were sold fat at about the age of 2½ to 3 years at Ashford Market and would make in the region of £5 to £7 per live hundred weight and weigh 12 to 14 cwt each.

Sometime during the War the MAFF introduced a scheme whereby a farmer could get an annual premium to keep a bull for his own cows, but had to make it available for the use of neighbouring farmers. One of the rules of receiving this premium was that someone had to be present at the farm where the bull was kept until 2.00pm each day. In its early days it was quite a successful enterprise, but when artificial insemination became available from 1948 the neighbouring farmers quickly changed over from the tedious task of driving their cows to the bull to the use of 'the bowler-hatted inseminator' (as we nicknamed him), who would turn up at the farm in his van, complete with bull semen.

Ten large white sows were kept, with some of their progeny being sold as weaners, but the majority were kept on to bacon weight of 210lbs. Along with most people, I had always thought that pigs were unable to swim, but one morning I was helping the local carrier load some weaners to go to Ashford Market when one of them escaped. He made a beeline for the adjoining pond, slid down into it and swam directly to the opposite side, a distance of about 30 yards. When he walked out of it he shook himself, just as if he was used to taking a regular morning dip!

During the summer of 1951 I asked Mr Gordon Jones for permission to start a small chicken rearing unit on my own account. This request was granted gladly and I was wished the very best of luck.

This was the start of my own farming enterprise. I purchased the body of an old army truck and built a roof on it with some plastic windows. It wasn't a particular thing of beauty, but in the 10 years that it was used I managed to rear about 16,000 pullets in it. The Miller Brooder that I installed took 150 chicks at a time, and after four weeks they were transferred to haybox brooders which were situated in the orchard where the brooder house stood. I readily found a market for these pullets by advertising them in the *Kent Messenger*. The price I received for them was one shilling per week of age, with the majority of them going at eight weeks. During the 1950s, unlike today, most farms would carry a small laying flock of hens and found it more convenient to buy in their replacements than to rear their own.

July 2nd 1952 was a day of great joy for Mary and I, for that was the day that Rosemary was born. During the afternoon a batch of day-old chicks arrived. Mary had got them settled into the brooder when she suddenly got the feeling that her offspring was getting a little bit impatient to enter this world a few days earlier than had been forecast.

When I arrived home that night after a busy day's haymaking, I was quite surprised, and a little bit alarmed, to find the midwife's car in the yard. After a short while she decided that she would like the services of the doctor. He arrived about 11.00pm a bit the worse for drink. (He wasn't our regular doctor but a stand-in.) The midwife was rather alarmed with his condition and asked me to keep an eye on him! He had occasion to need the use of his forceps, but realised that he had left them in his car, and set off down the stairs to collect them.

The midwife asked me to follow him in case he lost his way or another mishap befell him. With the lighting arrangements being a little on the sparse side, I was able to keep at a safe distance without him observing me. As I arrived at the bottom of the stairs, there he was with the front door open, standing on the porch steps having a well deserved pee. When he had adjusted himself he started to climb back upstairs and, on my stalling his progress in the wrong direction and telling him that he was unlikely to find his car up there, he said, "Damn it lad, I am much obliged to you for reminding me the reason why I was down here."

The following morning all was well, Mary's mother and father arrived with Mrs Rout who was to help in the next few weeks. With my nursing skills no longer being required I went off to work, but on coming home to dinner at 1.00pm I was beginning to feel drowsy, not having had a lot of sleep during the night. With all the activity that was going on indoors, and not being able to find a quiet corner to settle into, I found myself having a rest in the hay barn and dropping off to sleep.

Margaret, our second daughter, arrived in nearly as big a hurry on the morning of 1st August 1955, which was a Bank Holiday Monday. Mary, Rosemary and I had been to Pett Level the previous afternoon, where Mary had taken a swim and I had paddled in the shallows with Rosemary. All went well, without the worry of a half-tipsy doctor to contend with! They were very happy days, seeing the girls grow up and eventually go to the village school in Biddenden, walking there across the fields and enjoying the 20 minute journey.

Among our Christmas mail in 1952 was a letter from my sister Edith who with husband Sandy, nephew David and niece Pam, my godchild, lived near the Moray Firth in Forres. She suggested that with the Coronation of Queen Elizabeth 11 coming up in early June 1953, might we view it together in London. I was highly delighted with this suggestion and, after conferring with Mary, we decided that it would be a shame for one of us not to watch such an historical event.

During the morning of 1st June 1953 Mary and I drove up to London in our rather ancient Morris van, with Rosemary just 11 months old sleeping in her carrycot in the back. After leaving them all with Gran and Grandad Burt at 33, Middleton Road, I went on to Kings Cross Station to await Edith's train from Scotland in the early afternoon. Edith had worked out our campaign of viewing which was to be in the Mall. On our arrival there at 3.00pm the crowds were beginning to assemble and we were able to pitch our spot about 30 yards on the Mall side of Admiralty Arch.

This position turned out to be a superior vantage point for the full 24 hours that we occupied it. All the people were in a very joyous mood and remained so through the night, in spite of the light rain that persisted in the early hours. Edith and I had brought raincoats with us so we got off quite lightly, but the majority of the onlookers had to rely on the London evening papers (which were in plentiful supply) to help keep dry. Most of them were reluctant to leave their spot for fear of it being readily occupied by incomers.

Before leaving Scotland Sandy had advised Edith to forget about taking anything to drink other than a bottle of whisky. This bit of advice was invaluable as a low intake of liquids considerably reduced our need to spend pennies.

Early in the morning of 2nd June the Mall became a scene of intense activity with the Military very much in charge of the operations. The excitement of the crowd is something that is hard to describe. If my memory serves me correctly the Royal procession set off from Buckingham Palace at 11.00am down the Mall en route to Westminster Abbey for the Coronation. As the procession advanced down the Mall the very loud cheers from the crowds got increasingly louder. The Gold Coach, drawn by six magnificent horses, carried the Queen and Prince Philip who acknowledged the cheers from the crowds lining both sides of the Mall.

The procession that followed the Gold Coach stretched for a long distance with most members of our Royal family and many overseas heads of state. The most impressive of all was the very colourfully dressed Queen Salote who ruled the Island of Tonga in the Pacific Ocean. She was the sole occupant of her carriage and just about used up all the seating space. She bowed and waved to the vast crowds who cheered her on with much enthusiasm.

Edith was so pleased with our exciting day and has talked about it many times since. On the morning of the Coronation another historical occasion was announced to great cheering from the crowd. Edmund Hilary and Sherpa Tensing had reached the summit of Mount Everest, the first to do so.

10. Sheep May Safely Graze

In October 1956 I bought my first lot of Kent wether lambs in Ashford Market. I had acquired some winter grazing on a farm at High Halden, on which I would be able to keep 30 lambs until mid-March. On selling them to a local dealer, Dick Offen, they left a small profit. From these small beginnings I gradually built up quite a flock, numbering close on 500 breeding ewes. By 1962, the year that we left Randolph Lodge, 250 of these ewes were on a farm at Uplees on the marshes alongside the River Swale. The owner of the farm had advertised this grazing on a profit-sharing basis, with him supplying labour and feed. In return for this, he received all the money for the wool and half the proceeds from the sale of the lambs, with me getting the other half. I was also responsible for the depreciation of the ewes and rams. Mostly I bought Kent ewes that had already produced three crops of lambs, mainly because they were much cheaper than ewe tegs, and secondly, because they didn't need quite such close shepherding at lambing time on those very exposed marshes. This area had been flooded for quite a period during the great coastal floods of 1953, when the whole of the coast suffered. The salt water that breached the seawall had severely affected the grazing on the marshes, hence the fact that nearly 400 acres just about supported 250 ewes and lambs. The rest of the flock were kept locally where I had been able to obtain grazing. The method of payment was chiefly in the form of a headage fee, which most of the time was one shilling per ewe per week and a further nine pence per head for the lambs from September until they were sold. I managed to get help with the lambing in the form of casual labour, as I was still working at Randolphs.

In 1961 Mr Gordon Jones died, followed by his widow the next year. The farm was to be sold and Mary and I, with financial help from her parents, were keen to buy it, but alas, when it came up for auction, the price exceeded our budget and dashed our hopes of getting it. The sale took place in May 1962 with possession in October. This gave us five months in which to find a farm to suit our pocket. Having built up a string of local grazing arrangements, we wanted to get something in the area, with the idea that we would be able to carry on the business that we had worked so hard to build up. With not many farms coming on the market at a time of stability in the farming industry, we were lucky that

White House Farm came up for sale, just in time for us to buy and occupy it on 12th October 1962.

At that time the farm consisted of 38 acres of land with the house and buildings. The house dates back to the mid-19th century with modern extensions being added in 1950. The farm buildings were built at that same time though they bear no resemblance to the ones that exist today.

It was with a certain amount of sadness that we left Randolph Lodge Farm after spending 12 happy years there working for the Gordon Jones family. On leaving, the executors handed me a handsome cheque in appreciation of my years of service with the family.

A herd of 10 Jersey cows had been run at White House Farm by the previous owner, who was the fifth occupier of the farm since 1940. The herd had been sold in the spring of 1962 and the farm looked rather sad, having become run-down as a result of under-grazing. In the late 1950s the MAFF introduced what was known as the Small Farmer Scheme which remained in existence for about eight years. I agreed to participate as I saw a way of improving the farm by ploughing and reseeding it back to grass over a period of three years. The ploughing grant was £7 per acre for each of the three years that this plan was in operation. I hoped to raise the stock-carrying capacity of the farm, a target I readily achieved. In October 1962 a local contractor ploughed the whole of the farm except for just one meadow. It was drilled with Cappele wheat, which in turn rewarded me with an average yield of 41 cwts per acre, which was well up to expectations for that time.

The winter of 1963 proved to be one of the worst of the century in Kent, and many other parts of the country too. The first heavy snow fell on 27th January and was followed by several other falls, with most of it laying until mid-March. That winter I had increased the ewe flock to around 350, plus I had the marsh flock which suffered quite heavy losses, amounting to 20% of the total. My days were mostly spent carting hay out to the sheep which were out-to-keep on five different farms. By mid-February I had used up all my hay and had to go out and buy some at the high price of £10 per ton which I collected from a snowbound barn in Pook Lane.

For reasons of strict economy I had delayed the purchase of a tractor until funds were a little more plentiful. My only mechanical power during that first winter consisted of the Operman moto cart which was in its 15th year and had been used for all kinds of carrying work during the years that I worked at Randolphs. It must have carried many thousands of bushels of fruit from the orchards during that period. The executors wanted me to have this machine on leaving their employ and, by mutual agreement, it changed hands for £10. I used it for a further four years before selling it at a small profit. Now you may wonder what this moto cart looked like, as I think they were only in production for about five years, with the last one being built in 1952. It was a three-wheeled vehicle with the single driving wheel in front, a well for the driver to stand in and flat bed at the rear for holding the load which could be anything up to 30cwts. It was powered by a single cylinder 10hp petrol engine, mounted alongside the large front wheel. This engine made a delightful, loud, popping noise and whenever it was driven past John Mayne School in Biddenden, and it happened to be playtime, the children would crowd to the rails, and wave and cheer it on its way. I think some of those children, now in their 50s and 60s, will remember this odd machine.

The 38 acres of White House Farm were divided into 10 different fields, most of them enclosed by very overgrown and neglected hedges, and ditches to match them. As soon as the first harvest was cleared, we grubbed out several of these hedges with the help of a contractor, and reduced the number down to six fields. The remaining ones have been trimmed each year since then, firstly with a pneumatic, handheld cutter bar and, since about 1967, a flail hedge cutter has been used. The first time that I saw one of these flail cutters at work I was a little bit dubious about the aftergrowth of the hedge, but must admit that this machine has turned out to be the saviour of the much-neglected hedge rows in this part of the country.

For many years Michael Palmer, now our immediate neighbouring farmer, and a late student of mine in the early '70s, has done all our annual hedge trimming, and what an excellent job he makes of it.

In the autumn of 1963, following the death of Vita Sackville-West of Sissinghurst Castle, 19 acres of her estate which were adjacent to White House, were put on the market and I was lucky enough to buy it at less than £100 per acre. The reason for this very satisfactory purchase price related to the fact that it was sold with the agreement that two acres of the land was to remain in the occupancy for the life of the tenant, Tom Noakes, who had farmed the land since the early 1920s. Tom was a very outspoken man and his immediate neighbours were very much aware of this, hence their reluctance to show any interest in acquiring the land with this agreement hanging over them. Tom was a victim of the First World War in which he had lost his right arm during trench warfare. He was issued with a wooden one which lasted him for over 20 years, but

119

its replacement Tom described as "bloody useless". He set to and made his own which was quite a work of art, and he used it until his death in 1965. After his death the tenancy ended and I took over the two acres which were in a very sad state. It had been planted over the years with many species of soft fruit and apple, pear, cherry and plum trees. There were also numerous wired-in chicken runs. In his declining years the whole lot had become a sorry sight and it took me quite some time to clear it away. Tom had built the wooden hut that still stands on this land today, to move into if his sister, with whom he lived, predeceased him.

Prior to the lambing season of 1964, I was discussing with a neighbour the fact that I had had to buy a lot of milk during the disastrous lambing of the previous year. He suggested that he lend me a cow for a couple of months. This proposal was readily accepted and during those months the family became very fond of Buttercup, for that was the name she acquired, and we were rather reluctant to allow her to go back to her owner.

On hearing this, Keith Wooliams being of a kind nature, said, "Alright Stan, give me a cheque for £45 and she's yours". The offer was not rejected. She was three months in calf, and in due course presented us with a lovely heifer calf, Daisy.

1964 turned out to be a much more favourable lambing season than the previous one and the need for supplementary milk was much less. This meant that Buttercup presented us with a surplus of milk. Mary came up with the idea that she could skim the cream off it and sell it at the farmhouse backdoor, which she did very successfully with the use of a small hand skimmer. After a few weeks of this operation we were lucky enough to purchase a hand-powered Lister cream separator which Mary used for a few years before purchasing our first electric-powered one. This cream was sold in 1lb jam jars until plastic cartons were introduced, much to the dismay of some of the customers who preferred to see the rich golden cream through the glass.

During the summer of 1964 I finally made up my mind that the only future for this small farm was to develop it as a dairy farm, with the sheep remaining as the other main enterprise. There was a 10-stall, model cowshed ready for use, complete with milking pipeline and vacuum pump. The only equipment that I needed to acquire was a couple of milking units, which I soon acquired from a friend who had just retired from milk production. It was close on 20 years before the word 'quota' was even thought about in the dairy industry, and I well remember making a telephone call to Unigate Dairy in Headcorn on 31st

August asking them if they would start collecting milk from the farm. The very next day they arrived for my first churn which contained just two gallons of milk. Looking back to those less intensive days, I feel so glad that I didn't have all the hassle that is prevalent today.

I quickly filled up the 10 stalls with Jersey cows and also bought some heifers to join the herd which would expand to about 30 cows in the autumn of 1965. The 10-stall shed was not suitable for the larger number of cows that were to be kept and I decided to have a three-abreast milking parlour fitted into the existing cowshed. This alteration was the cause of quite a bit of upheaval. A temporary stall surrounding a large hayrack was fitted with a vacuum pipeline made with a length of hose and this set-up saw us through the transition period. The setting-up of the parlour was done by Lister and Pyecroft, with the Drury brothers laying out the floor - and me acting as their labourer. The adjacent collecting yard and feeding yard, complete with tombstone mangers, was completed with the same labour force. These mangers, which are now nearly 40 years old, are still in good condition, thanks to an annual coat of creosote in their early years.

I will take a break now from the erection of buildings and the purchase of Jersey cattle, and write about the border collies that have been a great help to me and the whole family over the years. They have all been bitches, chosen for their desire to remain at home, unlike some of their male counterparts. Floss, our first border collie, was just eight weeks old when she came to join our household in early 1951. Pat, Mary's red setter, readily took to this energetic puppy and they became the best of pals. The kitchen at Randolph Lodge was their night-time quarters. Every morning, Floss would follow me out and in a very short time she learnt to remain at my heels until further orders. I was often asked how I had trained her to be such an obedient dog and my answer was that she trained me, not the other way round.

Before she was a year old she would hold the flock of sheep in any corner of a field, allowing me to catch an individual sheep that needed attention in one form or another. Sitting down in the kitchen one day, eating our lunch, a knock on the door revealed Bob Ward standing there. "Stan, that young dog of yours is holding my small flock of sheep quietly in a corner, and no way is she going to take any notice of me to get her away from them."

I went back to the field with him to call her away, which she did immediately. Bob was so impressed with her response that he made me a good offer to buy her, but it fell on very deaf ears.

At that time, once a week, I was in the habit of driving the Operman moto cart down to River Hall Farm to collect a load of baled straw. Before leaving the farm I would give Floss strict orders to stay at home which she did, until one day she must have thought she was missing something good because, lo and behold, when I got round to Randolphs, which lay at the far side of the village, there was Floss sitting in the gateway waiting for me. After this I took a chance and let her accompany me on my trips and, when the load was complete, I would give her a leg-up onto the load, which was always six courses high, and that was the start of several years of her company on all my journeys.

When Floss was three years old she presented us with four lovely puppies, three dogs and one bitch. This happy occasion wasn't the result of any planning on my behalf, but the outcome of a night-time visit by the working collie belonging to our immediate neighbour, Dick Offen. The three dog puppies all went to good homes and were very highly thought of by their new owners.

Gyp, the bitch puppy we chose to keep, was almost a complete replica of her mother, but she never quite reached the extremely high standards of Floss. They were great companions and sometime in the middle '50s each gave birth to a litter of puppies, Floss five, and Gyp just the one, born within a few days of each other. Both of the mothers shared a cosy nest in the straw barn and all the puppies suckled from either of the mums without any jealousy at all. These pups were all sold to local families, mostly as pets.

Margaret kept a couple of white rabbits and it must have been about 1965 when one of them gave birth to a litter of young. Sadly, the mother died when they were about a week old, so they were installed into the warm cupboard adjacent to the Aga cooker in the kitchen. Margaret soon had them feeding on milk with the aid of a fountain pen filler. One day when she was feeding them Gyp, who was sharing the hearth rug in front of the Aga with her mother, started to lick these baby rabbits who became very fond of her attention. After a couple of days of this endearment Gyp lay flat on her back and the babies climbed onto her tummy and played for ages; it certainly was a sight to remember to see them running races the full length of her body. At the weaning stage these youngsters were passed on by Margaret to some of her friends.

I have many other happy memories of Floss and Gyp, one of my favourite being the time that we went to North Wales on a short holiday. In the village of Betwys Garrmon, whilst looking for a B&B sign, we came to an inviting-looking cottage. On asking the landlady if she had any vacancies for the four of us for just one night, she said yes. But requesting the freedom of her yard for the collies to spend the night in, brought a most definite no. With a little bit of persuasion she consented for them to stay in the car as long as we took them out for a walk both evening and morning. Early next morning Mary and I took them for a lengthy walk before returning them to the privacy of the car. After finishing our hearty breakfast the landlady came into the dining room and said, "Now, would you bring your two lovely collies into the kitchen," and to our amazement on entering the kitchen, there on the floor were two large plates, each containing a full English breakfast of two rashers of bacon, two sausages, an egg, a piece of black pudding and a couple of slices of fried bread. On seeing this lavish feast both of the dogs looked a little bewildered as they weren't used to this exciting fare at home. The good lady stood over them as they ate this meal and said she was so impressed with their immaculate behaviour that she couldn't resist giving them a treat!

Floss lived to the grand age of 16 years and Gyp 14 years. All the family were grieved at their passing. The next collie bitch was Lass, and following her was Meg, both of them good workers, but Meg was a bit scatty and had the annoying habit of chasing her tail which she never seemed to catch.

While the children were small we tried to take an occasional summer holiday. One, which turned out disastrously, occurred in 1969, just after we had inherited a rather fine car from Mary's father.

When he died in 1968, he left her his Armstrong Siddeley 17hp touring saloon, which had been his pride and joy since he purchased it new in 1935. This was the car in which Mary passed her driving test at her first attempt in 1938. It was a very sedate car, with real leather seats, painted green with black wings and a substantial luggage rack that folded down at the rear.

Having never owned any vehicle other than a van it was quite a step up in the world for us to drive such an attractive car. It was only used for local journeys as the petrol consumption was almost double the amount used by the Ford van in use at that time.

We had planned to spend our holiday in Scotland. We set off on this trip in late-July. After spending a night's B&B on a farm near Alston, the highest town in England, we headed for the border into Scotland.

We were driving towards Gourock, from where we intended to take the ferry across the River Clyde to Dunoon in the county of Argyll. It was raining steadily as it mostly does in the west of Scotland. A couple of miles out from Wemyss Bay, a large van travelling at about 50mph overtook a car and hit us head on. With the seawall on my left the only action I could take was to come to an abrupt stop. Thus ended our planned holiday.

Margaret was sitting in the rear seat and escaped any major injury. Mary also sitting in the rear, received a rather severe cut to her forehead which needed several stitches. Rosemary lost a tooth and received several bruises. I fared the worst with five front teeth left hanging from my gums but, worst of all, my right knee was completely shattered by the impact of the steering wheel column being driven off its base. The driver of the van and his mate suffered quite a bit of damage to their persons and the vehicle. The very kind resident of a house on the other side of the road, with the help of several of her neighbours, took us into her living room and administered first aid to the best of their ability. An ambulance soon arrived, loaded all six of us on board and sped off to the Greenock General Hospital where we all received treatment.

Mary and the girls were kept in overnight and discharged the following day, but I was retained for an operation on my knee.

The following morning as I lay in bed on the ward, overlooking the River Clyde and the hills beyond, a nurse came around asking whether we would like a plate of porridge or corn flakes. With my five teeth still hanging to my gums and awaiting the service of a dentist the porridge sounded the more likely to be eaten without the aid of teeth! To my amazement, I was the only one in this ward full of Scotsmen to make this choice, but I completely understood the reason why when I received my dish of porridge. It was cold and the consistency of soft rubber, and one of the patients seeing a look of despair on my face, called out, "They only make porridge once a week and in the case of your portion that time has just about expired."

Mary's brother Tom was quick to come to our rescue on hearing of our plight, for which we will be forever grateful. He drove up from Essex the following morning and took the two girls to Largs, where the car had been taken with the aid of the police rescue team. Our luggage was taken out of the car, and to Rosemary's amazement, her tooth was on the car running board.

Tom then took Mary and the girls to Glasgow to board a train to Inverness, where they were met by Uncle Sandy and Aunt Edith with whom they stayed a few days before returning home at the end of their very disrupted holiday. Tom's school friend, Tom Carruthers, lived in Carruthers Town, Dumfriesshire. He ran a machinery recovery service and he soon had the Armstrong loaded and taken down to Kent. Sonnie Hall of Hammer Mill Farm kindly offered a spare shed which became its home until the insurance was sorted out to our satisfaction.

I stayed in Greenock for six days before being transferred to Linton Hospital, a branch of the Maidstone General. Without being too much of a bore I would like to describe this train journey. Quite early that morning the house doctor introduced me to Mrs Jordan, the lady who was to accompany me to Linton Hospital. She was a lady of advancing years and was feeling rather elated at being asked to take charge of me on such a long journey. Had I been Royalty I don't think I could have fared much better than on that day early in August 1969. Although I was able to walk with the aid of crutches she insisted that I was placed on a stretcher and carried into the awaiting ambulance, taken to Glasgow station and transferred to a waiting train bound for London.

My guardian, after a little persuasion, was allowed the occupation of a complete compartment just for the two of us as she wanted her patient to have complete peace on such a long journey. Although I had eaten a light breakfast on the ward, she insisted on me having another one on the train, as she didn't consider a hospital one was good enough to sustain me until lunchtime. The waiter was summoned and a three-course meal ordered. The porridge was a vast improvement on what I had been dished up in hospital. By now my teeth had been removed and I was able to do justice to the bacon, eggs and toast that followed.

The four-course lunch that she ordered was even more elaborate, with a half bottle of red wine to accompany it. On arrival at King's Cross Station we caused quite a disruption to the platform staff, but much amusement to a few onlookers. An ambulance had been arranged to meet the train and transfer me to Linton Hospital. Unfortunately, the train had stopped on the opposite side of the platform to the one I had been carried onto. With the door of the compartment not lining up with the exit door from the corridor onto the platform, I suggested to my guardian that I could use my crutches to walk, but no way was she going to allow me off my stretcher. After a heated discussion with the platform manager, with much embarrassment to myself, the window was removed and I was lifted out onto the platform and transferred to the waiting ambulance, to the satisfaction of the good lady.

We arrived at Headcorn Ward, Linton Hospital at 11.00pm. The ward sister welcomed us at the door and said to my escort, "You may leave your patient now." " Most certainly I will not," was the reply. "I will not leave him until I see him safely in his bed enjoying some light refreshment!" I must say how very grateful I was for her care of me on that long journey, in spite of the removal of the train windows!

After the operation on my knee I spent a further three weeks in hospital before returning home to find the farm in good shape, with the family coping very well. John, the relief milker, had settled in well and remained for five months until I was able to manage it myself.

As for the Armstrong, it would experience another adventure, of a more pleasurable kind, to which I shall return later.

During the mid to late '60s the dairy herd gradually increased to 40 Jersey cows. On obtaining the tenancy of Tanner Farm's 21 acres, and the Vane field which contained 15 acres of land adjoining White House, we decided to increase the herd still further to 60. Making this decision meant building an extension onto the existing cattle yard and feed area. This was completed in late 1970, along with the three-bay straw barn.

At this time of further development of the farm Mary was kept busy with the increasing demand for Jersey cream, for which we had now obtained a licence to sell direct from the farm. We put a notice out by the roadside informing passers-by that Jersey cream was available at the farmhouse. On a table under a small open window in the lobby Mary would place a cold bag containing several cartons of cream, ready for sale. Beside this bag was a pot into which the customers would place their money. In all the years that we sold our produce in this way we had just one rogue customer. On that day someone made off with all of the unsold cream, but left the money from previous sales intact.

Ian Sinclair, aged 13, whose mother was one of our first customers, was keen to earn a few bob for pocket money and suggested that he sell our cream on a small commission. He worked up a round of about 10 households, and each Saturday morning would arrive on his bike, collect the cream and cycle a couple of miles to deliver it to his customers. He returned with the money, collected his commission and went home a contented boy. Ian went on to become a student here in the '70s.

During those years of gradual expansion of the farm Rosemary and Margaret were a great help to me. One of the regular tasks that they carried out was the feeding of the young calves before setting off to school most mornings. In fact they helped in most things when and where they were needed. Lambing time, which I used to try and fit into the Easter school holidays for our mutual benefit, was always a scene of great activity from which they got a lot of pleasure helping with all the tasks involved. In those days lambing was carried out in the open fields, which in good, settled weather was preferable to lambing in covered yards. On plenty of days, however, when the weather turned foul any kind of shelter would have been more than welcome. For several years prior to housing the ewes, we lambed in the 10-acre field called Near Whatmans; the reason for this choice being the fact that it was a dry field with good hedges around it and it was free of ditches. Also, there were two small sheds which were very handy to house any weak ewes or lambs if the weather deteriorated. Immediately adjoining was Middle Whatmans to where we were able to draw the ewes and lambs when they were a few days old.

A ewe would select a spot in the field an hour or two before dropping her lambs and would remain in the vicinity for maybe 48 hours after their birth. I remember one morning finding a ewe with her two lambs near to a rabbit hole, about 20 yards out from the hedge at the top part of the field. A few hours later on a routine walk round the flock I could only find one lamb with her. After spending a little while looking for this second lamb and not being able to find it, I gave it up as lost, but after two more days the ewe was still wandering around this rabbit hole. Over the hedge, in my neighbour's field, there was a man out ferreting. I have always found it rewarding to have a chat with neighbours when the chance arrives, this being one of them.

"Stan, a little while ago my spaniel crept under the wire and started digging down a rabbit hole, but your old ewe wasn't too pleased with this interruption and soon chased him back, helping him on his way with a couple of body blows," he said. With this bit of information I decided to go and get a spade and investigate the hole. After digging for 20 minutes I eventually saw a lamb's tail and was able to get hold of it. On offering it to its mother who had come to watch the saga, she got very maternal and within 10 minutes the lamb was suckling its mother with much vigour. After spending three out of the first four days of its life down a rabbit hole it seemed to be in good shape, thanks to a feed of colostrum before its adventure.

During the 1960s a new idea of forage conservation was beginning to get publicity in the farming press. This was the 'Barn Drying of Hay' system and so I purchased a Lister diesel engine, fan drying unit in 1968. I was very impressed with the result of this venture in its first season. A tunnel was made in the centre of each of the three bays and the fan with its canvas ducting was moved from bay to bay as required. We started cutting the grass at an early stage, during the latter part of May. As soon as it was cut it was tedded with the 'Cock Pheasant' tedder, an operation which was carried out twice a day for a couple of days, before it was baled on the third day. It was always carted and stacked into the barn the day it was baled, because failure to get it in quickly would result in it heating up, plus because it was being baled in this very green state the bales could easily lose shape and become a nuisance to handle. It was a matter of trial and error before we got the bales to the correct density and weight for ease of handling.

I was so impressed with the extra performance of the dairy herd that I made up my mind to go one step forward with this form of hay drying. This involved building a three-foot-wide tunnel at the rear of the barn and mounting the fan drier at one end. Each of the three bays had a folding door from out of the tunnel which was opened as required, to blow air in. The bays were clad with lightweight, galvanised iron to a height of 18 feet and each one had a false floor fitted 18 inches from the base. This method of drying proved to be much quicker than the single tunnel system that was used in the first year.

We made hay in this way for 10 years, mostly successfully, but occasionally the weather cheated us and we finished up with some rather indifferent fodder.

David Morphett, who was a student here for two years, went on to Hadlow College and would come back and help out on weekends. On the morning of 1st June 1974 he mowed three acres of grass in the front meadow in glorious sunshine. That afternoon a freak snowstorm covered the meadow. The next morning saw the end of the snow and a heat wave develop, enabling us to bale the hay in tip-top condition on 5th June.

During the early '80s another system of forage conservation became popular, big round-baled silage, which is still one of the most important ways of conserving grass. In 1981 I had my first baled silage made with the aid of a contractor. It turned out to be a good product and I decided to get a baler of my own. Although the barn-hay drying stood me in good stead all those years, I could see that silage was going to enable me to grow heavier crops of grass with a more generous use of fertilizers, and to conserve it at the optimum time of maturity. With a 30% grant from the Farming Horticultural Development scheme I purchased a Class Round Baler in readiness for the 1982 season. This step proved to be a sound investment, not only did my own grass get mowed and baled at the right time, but also being one of the first round balers in this area, a number of farmers from the neighbourhood were keen to give it a try. At that time I had a very keen student working for me by the name of Robert Humphreys. He quickly mastered the operation of the baler and did all of our silage bales, as well as the wheat and barley straw we had from our immediate neighbours, T & M James, on an exchange deal. Not only did he do our own baling, but during the season he did several thousand bales of silage and straw for other farmers. Some days Robert would arrive back at the farm rather on the late side. I really had little to worry about as he delighted in telling me that he had picked up another customer and had baled a few acres for him on the way home. At the end of that first season the revenue from the baler just about equalled the full capital investment.

The exchange of straw for our farmyard manure started with our neighbours in 1967 and, with a few slight adjustments in the terms of transfer, still holds good in the year 2005.

As I am now over my four score years and my memory is beginning to wane, I hope that I will from time to time be forgiven for delving into the past. One very interesting period was the few years that I spent as a member of the Headcorn, Ulcombe and Boughton Malerbe farmers' discussion group. Early in November 1950 just after moving to Biddenden, on looking at the adverts in the *Kent Messenger*, I spotted a small announcement that the above discussion group would be meeting at the Who'D A Thought It at Grafty Green. Unlike the very much more modern pub that exists there today it was then an old-time country pub with quite an agricultural air to it. On the night of this meeting I persuaded Mary to come along with me as I was sure that some lady farmers would be present. But not a bit of it; one look into the small public bar which was crowded with only male farmers and she decided to go into the adjoining snug bar and wait 'til I came away at the end of the meeting, which as it turned out was close on three hours later.

I stayed a member of this group until it was wound up in about 1958. During that time I enjoyed the monthly winter evening meetings which were held in one of the local pubs, and also the few summer meetings that were usually on members' farms. One meeting that is quite vivid in my mind was on the subject of fodder beet which was a crop becoming quite widely used in the early '50s. The speaker was a farmer from East Kent who had been feeding this new root crop to his dairy herd for a couple of seasons with satisfactory results.

One of the members of the group who was born and had spent most of his early working life as a porter in the Spitalfields Market in East London had moved down to a smallholding in the Ulcome area. Apart from the various vegetable crops that he grew he had established a pig and poultry unit, and it was to this last enterprise that he got a wigging at this meeting. Being a true Cockney he was full of wit, and being new to the care of livestock was keen to tell us about the trials and errors that he had encountered in the short time that he had kept them. He had grown an acre of fodder beet and was proud to tell the speaker that he had started feeding it to his pigs. On being asked what form of protein he was using to balance the diet, his answer was, if you'll excuse the language, "Well, I have a few bleedin' dead hens most days and I just chuck 'em over to the pigs and they seem to do quite bleedin' well on it!"

Each meeting that he attended we could be sure of a few humorous remarks about the activities on his smallholding. Eventually, I think that he went back to his old job at Spitalfields to enjoy a more steady way of life than he had endured on the smallholding.

Just a few members are still alive today. Looking back all those years to when I joined this club I was most grateful for the welcoming friendship offered to me as a newcomer from so many miles away. Four who come to mind are Charlie Gore, whose son George I see at hunt meetings and ploughing matches, sitting in his wheelchair and always willing to talk about those way back days. The others are Eddie and Geoff Chantler of Headcorn, who between them would bring life to any meeting with their different styles of humour, and Gordon Hodges who, with his wife, Flo, became long-time friends.

Another activity I grew to enjoy greatly was sea angling. Sometime in the 1950s Jim Luckhurst, an acquaintance of mine and also my barber, introduced me to this sport. He was a member of the East Hastings Sea Angling Club and, one Sunday morning in July, I joined him and two friends on a four-hour trip from the beach at Hastings in a sturdy, little rowing boat.

The previous afternoon I went along to the fishing tackle shop that used be in Tenterden High Street and asked the proprietor to fit me out with the bare necessities required for sea angling. After some time I walked out of his shop, carrying a sizeable parcel of equipment, such as a five-foot sea rod and a rather expensive reel, both of which I have to this day, half a century on, but sadly haven't used since the mid '80s. Among the other equipment were fish hooks of various sizes, and floats and weights for the different depths and currents of whatever area we would be fishing. I also purchased various cards of different gauges of line necessary for the type of fish we would be catching.

Being very aware of what all this was costing me, when the proprietor quoted me a price for a suitable canvas bag to house this tackle, I suddenly remembered my old naval issue, canvas, gas mask carrier, that was unused at home, and that cancelled out any further thoughts of buying a smart, expensive bag!

This first day's fishing turned out to be quite productive for me with a catch of 15 mackerel, a result of them being in abundance at this time of year in the English Channel.

After a few trips from Hastings I went out with Mick Bates in his 30ft diesel-engine cutter from Dungeness beach. These trips were usually fruitful with whiting, cod, dabs and the occasional dog fish being the most common catch. One memorable trip was when Mary and I, along with Rosemary and Margaret, ventured out on a bitterly cold day during the Christmas school holidays. With the wind blowing from the north Mick Bates took us round Dungeness Point where it was a little more sheltered, and anchored about half a mile out from Denge beach. This proved to be one of the most productive days fishing that I have experienced, for when we got home that evening just over 50lbs of cod was gutted and put into our deep freezer. Much to our embarrassment, Mick and I had an absolutely nil catch, with the lady folk sharing the whole catch with tackle lent to them by Mick.

These fishing trips were very few and far between, with the farm becoming more developed. In fact there was a gap of a few years when I failed to get afloat. Ron Brunt, a neighbour, ran a small group of sea anglers and I was invited to join them whenever there was a vacancy. The boat from which we fished was based at Rye Harbour. How long we stayed out at sea was subject to the tides, which in some cases amounted up to 12 hours. Some days we went several miles out into the Channel and fished around old wrecks, in the hope of catching conger eels which frequented these areas, but I never witnessed one being landed. Cod was the main species available.

Back on the farm, during the early '70s I was looking for a small sideline away from milking cows and tending to a flock of sheep, which at that time amounted to about 300 breeding ewes. In 1963 I had acquired the tenancy of a two-acre field alongside the main road leading to Sissinghurst. Being a small area, without water and badly fenced, it would just be used for growing cereals.

This field was the answer to my requirements and the first year I planted it with FI hybrid courgettes and a small area with ornamental gourds, a crop which I had grown in the kitchen garden for a few years with a fair amount of success, so I thought I would give them a try on a field scale. Apart from the cost of the seed the only capital investment was one garden trowel. The inter-row cultivations were done with a Howard Rotavator, kindly lent to me by Vic Payne, a close neighbour, and in return for the use of this machine I used to take him half a dozen loads of muck for use in his own one-acre vegetable patch which he kept in immaculate condition. The courgette crop was quite good and was sold in one or other of the London markets, according to the one that Jim Larking, the carrier, was attending on that day. The gourds were sold in a few local shops, with Webb's of Tenterden having the largest turnover. The following year a quarter of an acre of these gourds were grown from seed obtained from a Dutch seed merchant. Growing plants from this superior seed resulted in a much greater variety of shape, colour and size of gourds. I was able to pack them into Dutch trays, 25 to a pack, each different. With a clear polythene cover they looked attractive and sold extremely well at Covent Garden Market. The success of this very satisfactory sale must have made me a bit bigheaded, as the following year I planted the whole two-acre field with gourds. As it turned out, that was a very good growing year, but alas, when it came to marketing them things didn't go at all well. The merchant at Covent Garden told me that there was a limit to the amount that he could sell and advised me to try some of the other markets. I did, but with very limited success and finished up ploughing in most of this bumper crop. That was the end of gourd-growing as far as I was concerned, having kidded myself that I was the country's largest grower! On the few occasions nowadays that I look in florist shop windows I have noticed that these rather unique objects are making a comeback, but I haven't been tempted to persuade the family to give them a second try. We carried on with courgettes for a few more years.

The spring and summer of 1976 turned out to be one of the driest on record and it resulted in us being very short of grass, both for grazing and conservation. We were without any measurable rain from February until the second week of September. When the rain did arrive, the soil was so warm that the grass sprang into life and resulted in a very pleasant autumn, with abundant keep from then onwards.

During September Colonel Lochhart telephoned me and asked if I would like to rent the land at Washenden Manor, which consisted of 65 acres of permanent pasture. Nearly at the end of the drought, the land looked so dry as I walked around, but I decided to take a risk and agreed to rent it on a 360-day, grazing tenancy. 29 years later we still occupy this land. It has been grazed entirely with sheep, numbering about 260 ewes and their lambs. It was about this time that I changed the breed of sheep that I kept, from the docile Romneys to the North Country Mules which, being a much more adventurous breed, tested the existing fences to the limit, resulting in quite a bit of work and wire-netting to get them stock-proof. The wayward antics of these mules at least gave me the opportunity, on collecting them back from my new neighbours, to discuss the better points of the breed and to hear their views, which I may say were not too complimentary.

Margaret helps to move some sheep

White House Farm

Ewe flock in its
winter quarters

Jersey herd
at rest

Rosemary brings in a new-born calf with mother following

11. Visit To New Zealand

The nineteenth day of August 1978 was a beautiful summer's day for the wedding of Margaret and Shaun in All Saint's Church, Biddenden. Many of our relatives and friends were in attendance and afterwards joined us for the reception at Bethersden Village Hall. On returning from their honeymoon they took up residence in a third-hand caravan which was situated in the yard here at White House Farm. A few months later they moved into their first house outside Headcorn.

In 1976 Rosemary had given up her job with the Hereford-based farm accountancy firm where she had worked since her year in New Zealand. She had spent a very enjoyable time in that country working on farms on both islands. Now she had come home to our farm and it was great to have her help. Her tales about this fine country rather whetted our appetites to visit it. One day early in 1978 she suggested that she felt quite capable of looking after the farm if we would consider taking the holiday of our lifetime. Mary and I readily accepted this kind offer and quickly booked airline tickets to take us on a worldwide trip, with New Zealand being the main stop. On 18th November 1978, after a nine-hour delay at Heathrow owing to thick fog, we eventually got airborne and, after a short stop in Bombay, arrived in Hong Kong, where we stayed for a 48-hour stopover. I had always talked to Mary about this colony and vowed I would take her there one day, to see for herself what a fascinating place it was.

Alas, the Hong Kong we flew into that night was very different to the one that I remembered leaving 33 years before. Flying down onto the new runway that stretched out into the harbour, looking out at a million lights, was a complete contrast to the drab scenes I remembered leaving behind all those years ago. We made full use of our time there and, on the first morning, we had booked a coach trip around the island. However, the delay at Heathrow meant we were several hours adrift with the schedule and, as a result, we both overslept and only just managed to catch the coach. I can honestly say this was the only time I can remember going without my breakfast and I swore not to repeat the experience! The coach took us on a full tour of the island, calling at most of the places that I had seen during my occupation days. Aberdeen had been extended with all kinds of new buildings, including several massive skyscrapers and shopping complexes. My immediate thought on seeing this great change was that I wished they had left it as it was. But I have always been a bit of a stick in the mud!

We had a very interesting trip on a sampan around the harbour; two huge, floating restaurants looked very impressive from the front, but the rear view was quite an eye-opener, with hundreds of chickens accompanied by dozens of sides of pork, plus other joints of meat and fowl, being prepared for the chef's larder. We also had a ride on the famous Peak railway from where magnificent views of the island and the New Territories could be seen.

Our second day started with a trip on the Kowloon ferry which was, until the building of the tunnel, the main means of transport from the island to the mainland of China. An enjoyable trip around the New Territories terminated in a visit to a medieval Chinese village which was a great joy to walk around, in the company of a very knowledgeable guide who was proud to share with his visitors the history of the village. At the end of the tour we were taken into the village hall to partake in a feast, the like I had never seen before. A massive round table was laden with food of all colours and shapes, so bewildering that I did not eat any of it, but Mary tucked in and enjoyed it!

On our arrival at Auckland airport, we were asked a few questions going through customs; about the farm and our whereabouts since leaving the UK, the state of our footwear and a few more queries, all in the interest of protecting farming interests. A young Kiwi, complete with backpack, who I think was returning home from a season's shearing in the UK, was in the queue behind us. On hearing these questions he called out, "Don't take any bloody notice of him, he's got an old ewe at the bottom of his kit bag!" So much for the Kiwi humour, which we got used to during our 10-week stay in their country.

Before leaving the UK we had booked a rental car which was to be picked up two days after our arrival. Thinking that we would tour Auckland by public transport, we discovered that a bus strike was on, so we toured most of it on Shanks's Pony. On picking up our Ford Escort we headed north towards Warkworth to visit George Pendred's son and family with whom we spent two very pleasant days and nights.

Our next port of call was a dairy farm a few miles out from Waipu, where we were to meet Sheila and Bob Hodgeson. Sheila was one of a family who emigrated to New Zealand in the late 1940s and were friends of my brother Arthur, who had given us their address. On arrival at their farmhouse there was no one at home, but pinned on the back door was a note: 'Welcome Stan and Mary Lane, gone to cattle sale, back for

136

milking, go on in and make yourselves a cup of tea.' Typical NZ hospitality. We spent three pleasant days at their farm which comprised 280 acres supporting 240 cows, some Jerseys and Friesians, with quite a few Jersians which was a cross between the two breeds. I believe that this crossing ceased after a few years. The farm was on rather heavy loam which was excellent for grass. Just prior to our stay they had experienced excessive rainfall, resulting in the walkways to the dairy becoming a proper quagmire.

The high-volume water hose in the 24-a-side, herringbone milking parlour was used to wash the udders. The milking routine was quite a contrast to what I was used to at home, with Bob and his assistant pushing the cows through at such a rate. No concentrate feed was used at any time. We were shown around the processing dairy where the milk was used for the production of dried milk which was finding a ready market in the Far East. Whilst sitting eating our breakfast each morning a flock of about 25 wild turkeys would appear in front of the farmhouse, awaiting Sheila to throw them the scraps of the day. These small wild flocks were quite common on the farms in this part of Northland.

After leaving Waipu we headed for Paihia on the shore of the Bay of Islands, calling at Whangarie where we went to see Captain Bligh's ship, The Bounty. We stayed three nights in Paihia. On the first we joined a launch to go on the 'cream run', which was a trip all around the Bay of Islands calling in at any islands that supported very small dairy herds. In the past, the milk would have been separated and just the cream collected twice weekly, to go for butter-making on the mainland. It was a beautiful sunny day and the scenery was superb.

The following day we joined a coach party to the North Cape to visit the famous Cape Reinga Lighthouse, on the northernmost tip of New Zealand. On the return journey the coach driver suggested he take us down to Ninety Mile Beach which was quite a bit of fun with him doing a few motorized acrobats on this vast area of sand.

After leaving Paihia we set off south towards Ruakura and viewed the research centre where Rosemary had spent three months during her stay. We spent the night in Cambridge, rather a smart town with race horses being the main inhabitants, along with their owners.

Our next port of call was the farm of Dick and Mary Hall which lay about seven miles west of Lake Taupa. Dick, Sheila Hodgeson's brother, had emigrated at the same time as her and, after working a few years on farms, became eligible for a farm on one of the new land settlements. The farm he was eventually allocated was 400 acres of black pumice soil in an area noted for its earthquakes and close to some of the thermal springs. In the 20 years that he had been there, Dick had worked hard and made a superb holding out of the virgin land. The farm had no fences when he arrived, but now, eight separate paddocks had been fenced off with a central race running down to the sheep yard.

About 1,200 breeding sheep, all Romneys, were kept, along with a beef suckler herd of 40 Herefords. Extra store lambs were bought in for finishing off surplus grass as that part of the country enjoyed a good rainfall. I accompanied Dick to a local store sheep sale where he bought 500 Romney wether lambs to use up some of this surplus grass.

An interesting research project was being carried out on the farm. The black pumice soil was devoid of earthworms, as a result of volcanoes having deposited black ash over a large area. At a site 1000ft above sea level a patch of grass measuring 100sq.yds had been fenced off and scientists from Ruakura Research Centre had deposited a quantity of earthworms over this area. Each year they came and carried out a survey to record the distance that the worms had spread beyond the boundary and I think they were well pleased with the progress that the worms were making.

After spending a week at the Halls, and learning a lot about the local farming scene, we set off to Rotorua, the site of the most intensive thermal activity in NZ. We stayed a couple of nights in a motel complete with its own thermal bath where Mary and I had a good, hot soak.

Although this place was impressive, I still preferred the green hills and valleys that we passed through to get there. We had a very pleasant trip around the lake, close enough to the water to see trout swimming. It claims to be the largest colony of trout in the world and, judging by the numbers we saw, I can well believe it. Also on the lake were a group of 30 black swans which looked quite majestic, slowly swimming by.

Edgecumbe was our next stop, on the farm of Peter and Ann Withy, who were Rosemary's acquaintances. This was a very interesting farm on what had once been marshland, part of an area of 80,000 acres reclaimed from the sea in the early 1900s. Peter's grandfather had viewed it from the seat of a rowing boat supplied by the land agent. He was brave enough to buy 300 acres at a giveaway sum and set about draining it with the help of the Lands and Surveys department. Within 10 years it was capable of being cropped and fenced, a house was built and a milking parlour set up. The soil, being of a very alluvial nature, grew excellent grass for the 240 Friesian cows which were block-calved. During their dry period the herd were driven to a block of very rough land, situated several miles away from the farm. This inferior pasture was grazed for only about eight weeks, before the cows were returned to the home farm two weeks before the commencement of calving, with the paddocks having been well rested.

Some few years after our visit to the Withy's farm a very severe earthquake struck the Edgecumbe area and devastated their house, milking parlour and collecting yard. One of the Withy sons who came to work in this country was present at the earthquake. He told us about the complete chaos that his parents had to endure as a result of this act of nature. For the six months that it took to rebuild the house and milking parlour a kindly neighbour, a couple of miles away, let them use their milking parlour in between their own milkings.

After leaving the Withy's we headed across country towards Napier on the shores of Hawke Bay. This very picturesque route passed through the Waioeka River valley, giving us a good view of the gorge before reaching the twin town of Hastings, where we stayed a couple of nights. We had a good tour of the area where fruit and vegetables grow abundantly and where the many vineyards support an important wine-growing region.

On arriving in Wellington we had a good look around the city before catching a ferry the next day across the Cook Straits to Picton in the Queen Charlotte Sound. We stayed a couple of nights in this lovely small town and drove several miles alongside the beautiful sound, enjoying a fresh view at every turn… and there were plenty of them. We saw lots of quails and their chicks on the road verges.

From Picton we headed towards Blenheim and Highway Number 1, passing through vast vineyards, looking so neat and well kept. The drive down the east coast was a leisurely one, with very little traffic and lovely views; the Pacific Ocean on the one side and gentle rolling hills with many sheep on the other. We called into Hamner Springs, where we spent one night in rather a third rate camp, our only choice.

On then to the home of Jim and Olive Bennet, our one-time neighbours from Smarden, who had emigrated along with 11 other members of the family in the early '60s. Jim was farming in semi-retirement on a nice stock farm, a few miles out of Rangiora. He had always been engaged in dealing, mostly with sheep of various breeds, and always of top quality stock. He had been well known in Ashford Market, easily recognised by his smart appearance and button hole (usually a rose when in season). He took me along to the sale yards at Addington where we saw a lot of sheep and some cattle change hands.

Only one cow, a Jersey, was kept at the farm and Olive used to take her stool and pail down to the meadow twice a day to milk her, turning the milk into cream and butter.

Now in her 90s, she informed me in her annual Christmas letter a few years back, that she had ceased this pleasurable task and was getting her milk from the delivery van.

Jim had always been a great lover of Alsatian dogs. Remembering an encounter with one of them when I went to visit him at his farm in Smarden, I was a little alarmed to hear that he had three of them living in the house. There were also two puppies confined to the woodshed; they were in the 'doghouse' as a result of savaging a well-grown piglet. Now, at least once a night, I found it necessary to pay a visit to the bathroom. I dithered for quite a while, thus making the trip more urgent, wondering how I was to step over these three dogs sprawled across the corridor without being molested. Eventually, I plucked up courage and ran, or rather walked, the gauntlet. To my amazement, each of these ferocious-looking dogs just opened one eye, closed it and carried on with their snooze, and I must say that I got relief in more ways than one! This was the pattern for the three nights that we stayed there.

A few days were spent with Howard and Rosemary Bennet, on their mixed stock and arable farm at Rakaia. A week or so before our visit they had experienced some very high winds blowing from the west coast and, as a result, 12 acres of hay, almost fit for baling, had been blown against the wire boundary fence, clearing the whole field. Howard had almost finished forking this hay into his baler but he was mighty glad of my help for a few hours to complete the job.

A lot of the hay and alfalfa that is produced in this area is bought by merchants and transported to the high-rainfall area of Westland, to supply dairy farmers with the small amount of winter fodder they need. Owing to the excessive rainfall they find it more satisfactory to buy it in.

Howard, being a very keen fisherman, wanted to show Mary and I his favourite site on the Rakaia River where he had caught lots of salmon in the past. Much to his disappointment, heavy rain up-country had made the water too muddy for any angling.

From Rakaia we drove to Lake Tekapo in the McKenzie country, a very remote area of rather poor scrubland with many acres of wild lupins, foxgloves and viper's bugloss, a very pretty sight. We had seen them previously but nothing on this scale. At the end of the lake stands the delightful Church of the Good Shepherd. The large window behind the altar looks over the water with a magnificent view of the lake and mountain range, with Mt. Cook clearly visible in the distance. A little distance from the Church a stone statue had been erected in memory of all the sheep dogs that have played such an important role in the development of this remote area of the country.

The route from Tekapo to Gore took us through a lot of fine stock country to Cromwell, Alexandra and down through the Clutha River valley. We had been invited to spend Christmas with Kevin and Diane Kelly at their farm a few miles out of Gore. Rosemary had worked for them for a lambing season during her year in NZ. Although sheep were the main enterprise a red deer herd had been introduced with 120 hinds and 90 stags, and was still expanding, The antlers, more commonly referred to as velvet, were removed from the stags annually and were finding a ready market in the Asian countries for an aphrodisiac.

From Gore we travelled to Invercargill and Bluff Point where we caught a ferry out to Stewart Island, the southernmost point of New Zealand. Having visited the most northerly point at Cape Reinga we could now claim to have seen more of the country than most Kiwis!

On next to Te Anau, a rather attractive small town on the southern side of the lake of the same name. On our arrival in New Zealand we had made inquiries in Auckland about the chances of getting a booking for one of the walking tours of the famous Milford Track. Not a chance we were told as they were booked up months in advance.

On mentioning this to mine host at the guesthouse where we had booked in for a few nights, he said, "First thing in the morning, get yourselves down to the office where the walks commence, as they sometimes get last-minute cancellations."

Two mornings later we got a call telling us to be at the office and meet the rest of the party at 11.00am.

A guide took our party of 32 on a coach for 10 miles to Te Anua Downs, where we transferred to a launch for the remaining 12 miles to the head of the lake. The Milford walk was 35 miles, with three overnight stops in rather austere hostels. But plenty of good food and jolly company compensated for the rather hard bunk beds.

After spending the night at Glade House we started the walk, passing through some beautiful, wild country. The first day we followed the trout-filled Clinton River for nine miles, finishing at the hut at Pompolona.

Next morning, after leaving the Clinton River valley, we started to climb towards the Mackinnon Pass with the weather getting colder the higher we climbed. Our extra jumpers that we were carrying in our

141

haversacks now came into full use. On reaching the summit, a little above 5,000 feet, we were met with glorious views over the surrounding hills and rivers, well out to the coast. On our descent down the Pass we made a small detour to catch a glimpse of the spectacular Sutherland Falls, cascading 580 feet down into Lake Quill.

Quinton Hut was home for our last overnight stay. From here we made an early start for the last and longest walk. The first three miles of this 14-mile walk took us through more areas of beauty with Lake Ada on our flank. As we neared the end of the track, some horrid sand flies began to gather in ever-increasing numbers, making life most uncomfortable. We had encountered them in small numbers before, but now they had got past the odd bite or two, they had become a much talked-about pest. Luckily Mary had lost no time in buying a couple of bottles of repellent before we started.

Our walk ended at the head of Milford Sound, where we were met by a motor launch and taken to the hostel to spend the last night. We had heard stories of some of the walks having to be abandoned due to severe flooding in that area of heavy rainfall (with an annual average of 140 inches). But in our case we enjoyed superb weather every day without a spot of rain, for which we were more than grateful. Before we left Milford, as a final farewell, we were taken on a launch trip around the Sound and out into Tasman Bay. We passed close to the spectacular Bowen Falls and the 7,000 feet Mitre Peak rising to its full height from the water's edge.

On our return coach trip to Te Anau we went through the Homer Tunnel - a feat of engineering, with just under a mile hewn out of solid rock and a one-way traffic system. At Queenstown, where we spent a few pleasant days, we bumped into Don and Ruth Thomson, a couple of Australians whose company we had enjoyed on the Milford Track.

We made a visit to Arrowtown, a well-preserved historic town from the gold mining days. The precious metal was long since exhausted at the most prolific site, the Shotover River, and other activities had taken over - with vivid memories for Mary and me. Having been given a book of complimentary tickets by the car rental company to various top tourist attractions, we spent 30 minutes in what I thought was the highest insanity.

On a jet boat with six other people we wove about between the rocks at great speed and, just as we expected to mount these rocks, the driver had a knack of putting the boat into reverse, anticipating a capsizing at any second. Another exciting memory of the Shotover was our trip down into Skipper's Canyon, a distance of 17 miles. The track was only wide enough for one vehicle and several times I wished I could turn back along the track, but there was nowhere to turn. It had been hewn out of solid rock in the 1880s, purely for the gold prospecting in the river at the bottom.

Chinese labourers had been employed to build this ghastly track and it was quite sad to see that at the end a monument had been erected in memory of those who lost their lives constructing it, with sheer drops of several hundred feet for most of its length.

Another trip from Queenstown took us by launch to the southern shore of Lake Wakitipu and the Walter Peak station which consisted of several thousand acres of land rising from the lakeside up to over 6,000ft. It was stocked with both Romney and Merino sheep with only the latter occupying the higher levels. The mustering of these sheep on the steep mountainside was only possible with the use of helicopters. On arrival at the station we were surprised to see a herd of Highland cattle grazing alongside the water's edge, looking quite at home.

Next we headed for the west coast, passing Lake Wanaka and Lake Hawea, and over the notorious Hasst Pass which was suffering from severe rainfall and was on the point of being closed for traffic. We just made it only to find our road blocked five miles further on. A fallen tree had been washed down the River Paringa and had blocked a culvert, resulting in half a mile of road being flooded to a depth of two feet. Luckily, there was a motel a couple of miles back along the road and we were able to get accommodation for the night.

The drive up the west coast was of great interest, with the lowlands mostly used for dairy farming and the Southern Alps dominating the scene inland. On arrival at the area around the Fox Glacier we parked the car and walked as far as was safe up to this rather gruesome-looking landscape.

We left the coast road at Greymouth and headed towards Nelson. Some rather attractive fruit farms lay to the west of this city. The only hop gardens in New Zealand are situated in this area, though the oast houses that serviced the crop could hardly be described as desirable properties for conversion. They were all square and built with rather shabby weatherboard, with rusty, galvanized iron roofs. They would look rather out of place in the Weald of Kent.

From Nelson we headed back to Picton to catch the ferry to Wellington, passing through the beautiful Queen Charlotte Sound for the second time. Our first stop on the coast road was Himatangi to meet

David and Maureen, friends of Rosemary from her Wye College days. They were farming this dairy farm on a Share Farming contract, an arrangement quite common throughout New Zealand. After a couple of nights we passed through Wanganui with Mount Egmont as our target which reaches a height of 2,518 metres. The area surrounding it is really good land with many dairy herds in evidence.

Mary and I set off on the good road which winds nearly up to the summit, with the idea of getting to the top and taking in the view as we climbed. Unfortunately, a very dense fog set in with visibility down to just a few yards. We kept travelling for some time thinking it would clear, but no such luck, it got worse so we turned back. After spending a night in a comfortable motel we set off towards Napier via Manunui and through the Tongariro National Park. A few miles along the road we had occasion to stop and get out of the car, and looking back there was Mount Egmont in all its majestic glory, standing supreme in the glorious morning sunshine. With this sight we rather forgave the powers above for being cheated of it on the previous day. We had been warned of the uncertain weather pattern on the mountain.

Passing through Taihape, where I seem to remember getting a well needed hair cut, we took a most interesting road, passing through some wild mountainous country towards Hastings. It took most of the day to complete this trip of 140kms as the road was unmade and very dusty, with bends galore! Traffic was almost non-existent but a lot of agricultural development was being carried out on the more favourable hillsides, with Aberdeen Angus cattle being the most numerous of the livestock, along with some Romney sheep. About halfway along this road we came to the rather misquoted stretch of road called Gentle Annie, which we found far from gentle, but were so glad that we had the pleasure of driving over it. After two nights in Hastings we toured this very intensive and productive farming area with a wide variety of crops growing in the fertile soil.

Our next destination was to the home of Peter Reeves at Mokairau Station, about six miles north of Gisbourne. A couple of years prior to our visit to New Zealand Peter Reeves' eldest son had spent a season with a shearing gang in the UK and had been to our farm to shear the ewe flock. I seem to remember rain had stopped shearing for this one day and, to take their mind off the situation, I suggested that they may like to partake of a glass of my home-brewed cider. Not only did they enjoy this glass but were rather willing to give the next one a chance to see if it equalled the first. After several repeats they agreed that each one got better. Before the gang left the farm, in rather an elated state in the continuing rain, Peter handed me a piece of paper with his home address written on it and said, "Stan Lane, if you ever visit our country, you will be more than welcome to come and visit me and my family."

We had a most welcome three days stay here and were shown around by Peter and his family. The farm consists of several thousand acres of dry, mostly hillside grazing. At that time, in 1979, it was stocked with a large flock of Romney ewes which were crossed with South Down rams for the production of lightweight lambs, mostly for the export market. In addition, a substantial herd of Polled Hereford cattle were kept. A number of prize cards were decorating the woolshed wall, evidence of their success in the show ring, but the real pride and joy of Peter Reeves senior was his stud of purebred Clydesdale horses, which were a very rare breed in the southern hemisphere.

Our next move was to Hicks Bay on the east coast. This part of the country supports a large population of the Maori race, and it was interesting to pass their various styles of farms and other country dwellings.

Leaving Hicks Bay, we kept to the coast road that hugs the southern shore of the Bay of Plenty as far as Tauranga. We spent a lovely day touring round the Coromandel Peninsula, which boasts a number of small bays and several villages.

I remember when Mary and I were settling down to a picnic lunch on a spot quite high up, overlooking the Firth of Thames, with Auckland in sight on the mainland beyond. A lone cyclist rode along and, seeing us sitting picnicking in such an attractive spot, dismounted and asked if he could join us. He was a Catholic priest out for a pleasant ride on quiet roads. After the picnic out came his camera and, a few weeks after our return home, a photo of us sitting in this pleasant spot, arrived in the post, sent with his compliments and thanks for a pleasant hour with us, so far from home.

Our journey from Thames to Auckland passed through the most intensive dairy farming area that we had seen so far, with several miles of superb pastures, mostly being grazed with Jersey cows. One place of interest that I have failed to mention was our visit to the Stubb family, friends of Nora Bearsby of Frittenden, who farmed a very hilly and rocky station near to the Waitomo Glow Worm Caves. We were taken on a full tour of the station which was quite spacious. Sheep, cattle and a fair-sized herd of goats shared the grazing of this very rocky terrain. In the front room of their house stood a skeleton of a Moa, a gigantic extinct bird that was native to New Zealand. The various parts of the skeleton had been found in the early days of their settlement and they had assembled it in the house - quite an achievement. We also toured their own glow worm caves. Here we were so high up with a wonderful view, it felt like the top of the world.

Our last day in New Zealand arrived and, after handing in our baggage, we took a walk to the top of One Tree Hill, a well-visited beauty spot where the panoramic view of Auckland and surrounding sea and islands was superb. The walk brought to a close 10 unforgettable weeks in such a hospitable and beautiful country. Many thanks to all of you good folk who made us so welcome.

Our first stop was at the Fiji Islands before flying onto Honolulu where we passed through customs prior to entering the USA. Mary was rather upset when the nice little melon that she was carrying was confiscated by one of the custom officers, but even more so on returning to our seats on the plane to find that a couple of apples she had left there had also been taken.

After disembarking in Los Angeles we were taken by coach to Anaheim where we spent two nights as part of our package deal. Being just a few miles from Disneyland we thought we would give it try, really expecting it to be a waste of time, but how wrong we were; we spent the whole day there and enjoyed it like a couple of kids. We visited most of the main attractions with the Small World being the favourite. We were very impressed with the immaculate state of this vast pleasure area.

By chance, whilst breakfasting in the Draw Bridge Hotel we got into conversation with three American ladies who were attending a conference. They came from the Yokohl Valley in Central California and had interests in a large cattle ranch. Before we left their company we exchanged addresses and have since become close friends, with them visiting us, and in return, we have visited them on three occasions, which I will be talking about later.

On our return home it was good to see the farm looking so well under Rosemary's care and attention. Many thanks Rosemary for making this overseas trip possible. She had got the ewes safely housed, ready for lambing at the end of March. The Mule ewe lambs that I bought in the previous September were looking well and the cows enjoying the comfort of the well-strawed yards.

Rosemary and Mike were married in All Saint's Church, Biddenden, in November 1980. Unlike the beautiful sunny day that Margaret and Shaun were blessed with two years before, it was an atrocious day with high winds, heavy rain and puddles galore. James Chantler, our student at that time, set off after his early morning work and pestered some of his relatives to loan us six large umbrellas which were much appreciated. The reception was held in Smarden Village Hall. On the return from their honeymoon they stayed on Mike's family farm in Norfolk until joining us back at White House in 1984.

Clydesdale Stud at Mokairau Station, Nr. Gisborne

Kevin Kelly's deer herd

New Zealand

On the Milford Track, below and right

12. The Farm and Family Grow

In 1972 I bought my first batch of Mule ewe lambs and each year since then I have bought the number required to keep up the increasing flock size. This annual purchase came to an end in 2001 as a result of the serious foot & mouth disease that completely disrupted the movement of livestock for a considerable time. From then until the present time we have bought Mule ewe tegs as flock replacements. We also now have a large proportion of our own Suffolk X Mules in the breeding flock.

Mary and I went to Hawes in North Yorkshire to buy our Mule lambs at the sheep sales which are held on the second Monday and Tuesday every September. This is one of the most important couple of days for the farmers in that part of the Dales as about 36,000 Mule Gimmers (ewe lambs) come to this two-day sale, the first pick of their flocks. The price achieved for these lambs will determine their income for the previous year's hard work. Other sale yards in the North of England have similar sheep sales to those held at Hawes.

The popularity of Mules has grown enormously during the past 40 years and they are now one of the most numerous breeds in the UK. The main reason is their ability to produce a larger crop of lambs than most of the traditional breeds, and also the extra milk to suckle them.

Without boring you too much, I would like to say a few words about the parentage of these Mules. Our breed, the North Country Mule, is derived from the Swaledale ewe crossed with a Blue Faced Leicester ram. The prolific milking ability of these ewes is passed down from the Leicester rams. The Swaledale breed is very hardy and is kept mostly on the fells of Yorkshire, Cumbria, Northumberland and County Durham. After breeding the Swaledale ewes pure for their first three crops of lambs they are then moved down to more kindly pastures and the Leicester ram will be used to sire two, and maybe three, further crops of North country Mules.

The Scotch Mule is the progeny of the Scottish Blackface ewe and the Leicester ram, and the Welsh Mule comes from the Welsh Mountain ewe with the sire being the Leicester.

In all these years of attending the sheep sales Mary has accompanied me, and was such a great help with the book work, and helping identify the various lots that I had bought as they passed through the sale ring.

Seats around this ring were always packed tight with buyers, vendors and many onlookers.

Not only did we go to the Yorkshire Dales to buy sheep, but we also managed to take a few days' holiday. Over the years this area became one of our favourite parts of the country. I think we have explored most of the Dales by road, and quite a lot on foot, especially in the early days. One of our favourites is the walk from Tan-Hill, the highest pub in England down to Gunnerside in Swaledale, passing through the villages of Keld and picturesque Muker, where a fair is held in mid-September each year. We had the pleasure of being taken to this fair by Laurie Rukin, the owner of the farm where we stayed for a few nights.

Muker is a very compact village, close to the River Swale, with all the properties built from local stone. The fair field is on a slope, facing the river, with a quantity of hurdle pens, each holding one, two or three sheep of either sex, all of them purebred Swaledales. As this was one of the breed's main shows of the year it was conducted in a very serious atmosphere, with any celebrations reserved 'til later in the day.

The judging of these rather attractive animals was completed by 1.00pm and everyone retreated to the village hall to partake in a substantial Yorkshire lunch, washed down with some good ale. With the meal finished by mid-afternoon the prize giving took place amidst much cheering and clapping. The prizes all took the form of gold and silver cups which were presented by the President of the Swaledale Sheep Society, with a few words of praise and humour for the receivers of the cups. At the end of the session the Muker Silver Band took over a site in the corner of the field and played a variety of music, mostly classical, and it sounded supreme in this lovely setting, with the river close by and the fells beyond.

Fell running is a very important competitive sport in this part of the country, and we had the pleasure of watching one of these competitions take place. It was a lovely sunny day with the fells in full view of our vantage point. The 10 competitors started the run from the fair field, waded through the river, climbed quite a distance up the fell to where a tractor was parked and then ran 1½ miles across the top of the fell and round a second tractor that was sited on the summit. They then took a different route down the fell and traversed the river once more. There was much verbal encouragement for the leaders, expressed with the Yorkshire dialect at its best.

The village schoolchildren had their turn at the annual sports show at 4.00pm and gave a good account of themselves with all the usual races

149

being contested; the sack race being the most widely cheered, and the egg-and-spoon race almost as rewarding for the spectators.

The local ladies had prepared a wonderful display of home produce in their large tent; iced cakes, chocolate cakes, fruit cakes and many more, all of them looking much too good to meet the fate of the cake knife! Vegetables of all shapes and sizes occupied two long tables, the full length of the tent.

After supper we were entertained to some hilarious comic sketches by the local entertainment society, followed by dancing. Most of the people retired to the pub, The Farmer's Arms, to spend several more hours of revelry, with many toasts to be celebrated. Although our day at the fair took place over 30 years ago it was a day 'and the best part of a night' that will never be forgotten.

On 5th June 1984 our first two grandchildren were born, Alice and Peter, arriving in a little bit of a hurry, 12 weeks early. Thank God, they were kept safe and well in hospital in Norwich for several weeks with their mother, Rosemary, also remaining in hospital. In the autumn of that year Rosemary and Mike came to White House Farm and joined us as equal partners in the farm business, which has been a very satisfactory arrangement for these past 21 years.

Miriam, grandchild number three, was born to Margaret and Shaun on 27th October 1986, while Mary and I were on a farming tour in the USA. Lydia, grandchild number four, was born on 9th March 1990 in Aberystwyth so claims to be a Welsh National. In 1991 Margaret and Shaun and family came back to Biddenden. Mary and I consider ourselves so lucky to have all four grandchildren nearby.

In 1999 Margaret and Shaun went to Libya, to teach in the British school in Benghazi, with Lydia being their only British pupil. They found it interesting to experience life on the Mediterranean strip of northern Africa with a different climate and culture. Miriam spent the year as a boarder at school, but we enjoyed having her stay with us most weekends, sometimes accompanied by one of her international friends.

In the mid-'80s, a very serious disease struck our national cattle population, BSE, more commonly known as mad cow disease. This has been with us until the present day but is now occurring on a much-reduced scale and, hopefully, will soon be completely eliminated. It has cost the farming industry and the taxpayer a great deal of money. The cause of this disease has never been fully determined, but is widely believed to have arisen from the inclusion of meat and bone meal in the food, a practice that has now been discontinued for many years.

150

Within our herd we had several cows struck with this disease which was quite distressing.

The thought of farm fires has always been at the back of my mind and I am sorry to have mention the two that have occurred on this farm, one of them in 1991, but the more serious one in 1998.

On the morning of 25th August 1998 I had been down to Washenden Manor to do my daily lookering and, on my return, I was alarmed to see a fire hose connected to the fire hydrant close to the farm entrance, leading down into the farmyard. There was a scene of great activity: two fire engines and several folk were busy moving inflammable material which lay in the path of the fire. This was coming out of the barn that was stacked with large, round, baled hay in two of the bays, and about 12 tons of high-nitrate fertilizer in the adjoining bay. The fire, which we think was started by overheating, was breaking out in several areas of the stacked hay. Luckily the cows were all outside and the calves were removed from the fire area.

With considerable speed with tractor and fore loader, Mike was removing the burning bales of hay into the meadow immediately behind the buildings. Peter, at the tender age of 14, was driving the ancient Zetor tractor and loader, and was making an excellent job of removing the 24 half ton bags of nitrogen from out of the bay and depositing them well away from the smouldering bales. The third fire engine arrived by mid-morning and spent the rest of the day helping to put out this fire. Our neighbours were quick to come to our help and many thanks to Mark Scott and Hugh Richards for the unstinting help that they provided for most of that day.

When the fire crews had completed the final extinction of the fire, the farmyard looked a depressing site with the asbestos barn roof completely disintegrated, and all the steel girders and posts twisted into deformed shapes. It was some weeks later that we were able to get it rebuilt, and store the replaced hay that we had to buy.

The NFU Mutual Insurance Company, with whom all our business is connected, were very helpful in settling the claim for damages. They had sent one of their officials to observe the fire when it was at its height.

Despite BSE and the fires, the farm has prospered in recent years, owing to Rosemary and Mike's hard work. Three areas of adjoining land have come up for sale during this period and we have managed to purchase all of them. A fair amount of work was needed to bring them up to our standards, with fencing being one priority. All the land has been subsoiled, ploughed and reseeded, mostly with long-term leys. The farm now amounts to about 450 acres, including the rented land of Buckhurst, Washenden Manor and a few odd fields scattered around the parishes of Biddenden and Frittenden.

On this acreage we currently keep 130 cows, plus 100 followers of various ages and about 35 beef crosses. The sheep breeding flock is in the region of 700 ewes. Some of the best Suffolk cross ewe lambs are retained as flock replacements and the rest are sold at the lamb sales at Ashford Market.

For the past three years most of the wether lambs have been fattened and sold by auction on a live weight system, also at Ashford.

Alice, aged four, encourages a calf to suck

Left, Miriam, Peter, Lydia and Alice, 1991   Mule lambs 'gimmers' arrive from Hawes

Margaret, Shaun and Lydia, early April 1987

Left, Alice, Miriam, Peter and Lydia in Stan's naval hammock

Top: Alice (left), Rosemary and Mike on a hack

Left: Peter, after a successful shoot

Right: Shaun and Margaret

Below: Lydia (left) and Miriam in Bedgebury Pinetum

13. Farming The American Way

In October 1986 the Milk Marketing Board organised a trip to the USA to visit dairy farms in various parts of the country. Mary and I, along with 33 other farmers, started our trip in Philadelphia. Our first stop was a farm which was owned by a very wealthy car dealer, his main reason for farming being to avoid paying too much tax! His herd of Holsteins were top class animals and had been purchased at great cost. We were taken into the farm office with a semi-circular bay window, at least 50ft wide and 12ft high. This window overlooked the whole farm layout and the farm manager spent quite a while trying to convince us that this cow palace was necessary. It passed through my mind, and also others in the party, "Let's not see too much of this extreme luxury or we may as well have not come over here."

After leaving we were taken on a tour of the Amish country, a part of Pennsylvania settled by the Dutch in the 18th century. Farming is the main occupation of the Amish - and what an excellent job they make of it. The farms are mostly in the region of 100 acres, supporting a dairy herd. The Amish lead a very austere life with not many mod cons in evidence. Tractors, cars, telephones and electricity are not allowed in any form. All the lighting is supplied by oil lamps, no curtains are allowed and no vehicle can be powered by internal combustion engine. The only exception to this ruling is that diesel engines can be used to drive the milking machines. Horses are used for all the farm work and also to pull the various buggies and other domestic types of transport.

We had the pleasure of seeing two six-horse teams, each pulling tined cultivators breaking up stubble. A recent development intrigued us. A pick-up baler had been purchased and was being pulled by three horses, but the driving of the baler was done by an internal combustion engine. How they had got away with this luxury we didn't get to find out!

We dined in the Good and Plenty, the local Amish restaurant. The name was backed up by the superb, home-produced, plain food that we were served, and the speed with which the girls kept our plates topped up. They were dressed in attractive, old-type colonial dresses.

The next morning, still in Pennsylvania, we visited a high-yielding herd of Holsteins at Richlawn Farms. The herd average was 10,200kgs at 3.5% fat. We found all butter fat figures on the low side in all the states that we visited.

After a day visiting the sights in Washington we flew to Columbus, Ohio, and Select Sires, a co-operative owned by farmers throughout the US. This vast establishment housed 1,000 bulls, 800 of them Holsteins and the rest other dairy breeds. Angus and Herefords were their most popular beef breeds. Six Brahman bulls were also kept in this stud, the first I had ever seen. They are rather an attractive, dappled grey, with a huge hump above their shoulders and ears that droop down. Their main benefit is their ability to graze on dried-out pastures in hot climates and produce sufficient milk for their suckling calf. The semen from these bulls was used throughout the US, with 150 of them being progeny-tested for genetic advancement.

Our next stop was Select Embryos where 150 dry cows, all with very high merits were kept solely for the production of embryos which in turn were transferred to cows nationwide.

In Madison, the capital city of Wisconsin, we spent two days at their Dairy Show and Sale, which is regarded as the largest show of cattle in the World. 1,600 dairy cattle from all parts of the US and Canada were on show, with Holsteins in the majority. Brown Swiss, a breed that was new to me, put on a very impressive display, of which we had the pleasure to watch the judging. Both evenings we attended the auction sales in a massive saleroom and saw some mind-boggling prices obtained, with the top-prize Holstein selling for $230,000.

With an early morning start from Madison we had an interesting coach trip through fine Wisconsin farming country, this being the premier dairy state in the US. Maize and alfalfa are the most widely used crops for feeding, both green and ensiled.

We now flew onto San Francisco to visit four Californian dairy farms, As we headed out we passed through a vast area of dry semi desert with 300 wind generators dominating the bleak sky line, without any visible signs of habitation near by.

After spending a night in Modesto we went on a full day's tour of Yosemite National Park, passing waterfalls, mountain peaks and huge trees just beginning to display their autumn colours. The following morning began with a visit to a 7½ acre farm carrying 210 cows plus followers. They rely on all bought-in feed stuffs, alfalfa hay and concentrates. Our hosts at this farm had laid on a scrumptious barbecue for us, steak and all the trimmings with decent-sized glasses of Californian wine to help wash it down. The venue for this delicious meal was the very dusty farmyard in which our coach was parked, with its engine still running to power the air-conditioning. After a short time it had to be turned off to avoid us all getting covered in dust. On boarding the coach we did find it rather on the warm side with the temperature in the 90s.

The Harris Ranch was our next call where we saw one of the largest Beef Feed lots in the US, situated in the western part of southern California, well away from any sign of civilisation. It has the capacity to run 110,000 cattle on 600 acres at one time, but at the time of our visit they could only lay claim to 102,000. These animals are all bought in from the western states and Mexico. The desired weight on entry is 340kgs and they are sold at 500kgs after about four months of intensive feeding. They are grouped in units of 500, all completely in the open except for a sun-shaded area. The animals look extremely contented in these very low humidity conditions where average rainfall is four inches a year. Water sprinklers are situated all around the complex and come on automatically. A simple two-rail, feed barrier surrounds the enclosures and totals 17 miles in length, 15 mounted cowboys are continually monitoring the health of these animals and we were told that .05% losses were the norm.

By now we were beginning to wonder how much larger these farm units could become. We were not to be disappointed as we were now in the San Joaquin Valley which covers a vast area of Southern California and is considered to be one of the world's most productive farming areas.

During this visit, and two subsequent visits to this state, I have been amazed at the wide range of crops that are grown there. To name a few of them; citrus fruit of all varieties, almonds, walnuts, olives, pistachio nuts, cotton and vegetables of all descriptions, plus the ones I can't bring to mind. The low average rainfall of just six inches is supplemented with several thousand miles of water channels, a lot of them concrete-lined. The water from these channels supplies the irrigation that makes it possible to grow such heavy crops. The water is all channelled down from the snow-covered Sierra Nevada mountain range where it is held in large reservoirs, and systematically released when required.

Now to get back to the tour, which took us to Maddox Farm which consisted of 7,500 acres of dead flat, very fertile land in the valley. The Holstein herd of 3,500 cows, plus followers, had been established over the past eight years and were all enclosed in sand-based paddocks with a number of sun shelters, comprising a roof of light plastic. Four Herringbone parlours worked 24 hours a day, with a one-hour break for cleaning and maintenance between each of the three shifts.

This farm supplied all of its own forage. 3,000 acres of alfalfa was grown for producing hay and 800 acres of maize, which was chopped and ensiled. With the aid of irrigation and almost full sunlight for most of the day four or five crops of alfalfa could be grown each season. It was cut with a mower conditioner, left in the swath and not moved until ready for baling, the reason being to avoid the leaf getting shattered. The baling was done during the hours of darkness for the same reason. The bales were very tightly packed, weighing in the region of 120lbs.

The other major enterprise on this farm was 2,500 acres of grape vines that were grown for the production of Californian Sun-dried Raisins, a product that is widely available in most of our grocery stores. These grapes are harvested in a unique way. The vines are supported by horizontal rows of wires, spaced 6ft apart. Every 150 yards there is a 12ft wide alleyway, running at right angles to the rows of vines. A roll of reinforced heavy paper is rolled out between the rows and the bunches of grapes are picked and thrown onto the paper. They remain there for about 12 days before being collected. The paper rolls are connected to a specially designed machine that is driven down the wide alleyways. The machine gently winds in the paper rolls and deposits the raisins into the trailer following behind.

They are then taken to a large processing plant for cleaning and packaging. Several of these machines are used for gathering the large acreage of grapes.

Unfortunately, harvesting was finished by the time of our visit so we did not see the system in action. On being asked about the risk of rain damage, we were assured that they suffered only slight impairment one year in 10.

Our final day of farm tours took us to the Chion Valley, 50 miles south of Los Angeles. It is approximately 60 square miles and has the largest concentration of dairy cows in the world. After visiting three of these large herds we arrived at the largest of all, the Alta Dena dairy. Here, 11,000 head of Holstein cattle, including 7,500 milkers, are being kept on 250 acres of land. The feed for this vast herd is bought from a wide area, mostly delivered by rail to their own private railway siding.

One hundred and twenty five men, mostly Mexican, are involved in looking after the herd, with 95 of them working milking shifts in six Herringbone milking parlours. The standard of hygiene is very high on the farm, the only one with a licence to sell unpasteurised milk in California, which is available for sale in most of the large cities. Each milker has to have a shower and put on a clean set of clothing before his shift and, once a month, goes for a medical test. We were shown around the laundry, where three Chinese women were engaged in washing 30,000 towels each day; two for each cow for each milking.

Although the herd totals 7,500 cows, they are split up into groups of 120, according to calving dates and production levels. Each group is allocated 1½ acres of space, with one sunroof and sprinkler. The herd average for the previous year had been 8,200kg at 4% fat.

After the last day's entertainment at Disneyland the rest of the group set off back to England, very satisfied with their tour, but I rather suspect most of them were secretly longing to get back to their own less-intensive way of farming.

Mary and I stayed behind as we had arranged to meet our friends from Exeter, about 180 miles north of Los Angeles, where they have a ranch. We had met the two ladies, Bobbie and Gaye, in Anaheim on our way back from New Zealand in 1980. In 1985 they, along with husbands Harvey and Bill, had stayed a few nights with us during a visit to the UK.

The ranch is in the Yokohl Valley of Central California and Harvey had been the manager since the owner bought it in 1958. It consists of 39,000 acres, with elevations of between 200ft and 4,500ft. One area of it is completely bare of trees, with the rest fairly well covered with scrub and quite a lot of black oak. The rainfall is in the region of seven inches, which falls mainly from December to March. We were told that after the rain the landscape takes on a very different look, with wild flowers springing into life and pastures turning green. We have not had the pleasure of seeing it at this time of the year as our visits have been confined to the autumn. At this time everything looks absolutely dried up and it's quite astonishing how well the cattle look. The only supplementary feed the cattle get is *ad lib* molasses from ball licks attached to large tanks, situated in the more accessible parts of the ranch.

About 2,800 beef-breeding cows are kept, producing single, suckled calves which, after weaning at eight to nine months, are run on to reach live weights of about 300kgs, before being sold onto a feed lot to finish as prime beef.

Several breeds and crossbreeds of cows are kept, with Angus and Hereford the main ones. At the time of our visit the continental breeds were not being greeted with any amount of enthusiasm, I think because of their inferior ability to thrive on the steep hillsides and sparse grazing.

One hundred and forty bulls were kept on the only area of flat pastures and were fed purchased alfalfa hay for several months before being turned out with the cows about mid-December. The ratio of bulls to cows was one to 25, with several being held back as spares in case of lameness or any other problems.

Each morning Harvey drove Mary and I slowly along some of the tracks on the ranch, explaining the different stock-carrying capacity and other aspects of the 27 individual paddocks.

We saw some wildlife on our drives such as brown bears, coyotes and many birds, including eagles and, on one part of the ranch, hundreds of quail. Wild boar were seen on several occasions. Harvey was in the habit of shooting a couple of them each year to share the meat with his friends. I must say that I found this so-called delicacy rather on the tough side, very dry and without much flavour. It will definitely not be going on my shopping list!

Rattle snakes were quite common; although I saw plenty of their tracks where they had slithered over the dusty soil, I was spared the sight of one. Harvey told me that they occasionally lose a beast to a snake bite, usually inflicted on the nose whilst grazing in the dry grass.

Three cowboys form the workforce that takes care of the ranch, each occupying a house and a 10-acre paddock for their family's own use. Twenty ranch horses are kept in a large paddock adjacent to the main buildings. Each cowboy is allocated four horses for his work, with the remainder being kept for the use of outside helpers when necessary.

During our stay I was introduced to the game of golf. Apart from the occasional day's sea angling I had kept myself fully occupied on the farm and really had not given any time to outside activities. I have now become very fond of the game since I began playing in California but, alas, my handicap is still at the maximum, with little chance of me lowering it.

Some members of the Exeter golf club were going to a tournament in Las Vegas and Mary and I were invited to go with them. We drove 180 miles through a variety of landscapes, crossing into Nevada in the desert. Las Vegas is a very bright city, with night not varying from day. The brightly lit casinos are a hive of activity with punters from all parts of the world.

As Harvey, Bill and Bobbie were playing in the tournament, Gaye took us on a couple of trips; to the Hoover Dam and out to the Grand Canyon in the state of Arizona. We got out to the canyon reasonably early in the morning, which looked supreme with the sun shining down on the many coloured rock formations and the Colorado river flowing along the bottom.

It was on our last evening when we had occasion to telephone home to be told that Margaret had provided us with our second granddaughter that very morning, 27th October 1986, and both were doing well. Our American friends suggested that they gave a farewell party for us, and a greetings party for Margaret and baby Miriam.

Towards the end of this joyous celebration I felt the need to find the little boys' room. As I was leaving in front of the door was a one-armed bandit with arm outstretched, inviting all leavers to have a flutter! I slipped a dollar coin into the slot, pulled the lever and out rattled 23 dollar coins. During our stay at the Show Boat Hotel both Mary and I had played on various gaming machines - I had also played a few hands of Black Jack - with limited success. And so we bade farewell to our Californian friends, thanking them for such hospitality.

We arrived home to find the farm thriving in the capable hands of Rosemary and Mike, and our new granddaughter doing well, though still retained in hospital along with mother.

Having enjoyed this first trip to the US so much, we returned in 1992, taking a tour from Denver in Colorado, through South Dakota and into Wyoming. One night was spent in the Wild West town of Cody which is alive with the history of Big Bill Cody. A few miles out of town was a museum covering many aspects of his past life on the range, with old wagons, stage coaches, log cabins and much more. In front of the building was a very impressive statue to Big Bill.

From Cody we headed for Yellowstone which is the world's oldest National Park, and spreads to many thousands of acres, with the largest part-forested. Sadly, when we saw it in 1992, it was still recovering from a disastrous forest fire in the mid-'80s. Several thousand acres had been devastated but were making a wonderful recovery with thousands of young conifers growing amongst all the burned out trees, some of which were still standing in their black nakedness.

South of Yellowstone we took a raft trip along the Snake River. With the Grand Tetons as the backdrop this river is slow-running, giving us plenty of time to view a selection of wild life, including moose, elk, big-horned sheep and coyotes. Among the birdlife we saw bald eagles, heron, osprey, trumpeter swans and other species.

We then travelled on to Salt Lake City and visited the annual Utah state fair. In the main hall were vegetables of all descriptions and in the livestock section were numerous breeds of cattle and sheep, all of which were well groomed, much the same as we see in this country.

After a trip to the Grand Canyon, which we had seen on our first visit to the US, our tour ended in Las Vegas where, by prior arrangement, we met up with Gaye Crow and her sister Barbara who had a second tour marked out for us. This took us north into Nevada through the dreaded Death Valley that is so hot and dry that it is not a place I want to revisit. We then passed into Oregon where we took a most enjoyable jet boat trip up the Rogue River, and then passed into Northern California.

We bypassed San Francisco and headed down the San Joaquin Valley, viewing the great variety of intensive crop-growing in this very fertile area. We stopped at the area which the Californians claim as the Artichoke Capital of the world. I can quite see why, as a complete section (640 acres) of land is planted with globe artichokes which are marketed in rotation all year round. We were shown around some of the growing area and the spacious packing sheds, complete with cases of this luxury crop, ready for distribution to all parts of the States. We called at a large outdoor museum of farm implements that had been used in the development of the western states in the 19th and early 20th centuries. Here we ate the largest ice cream cornet we had ever seen.

Gaye and Barbara, who had given us such an enjoyable 2,000 mile tour, dropped us off at the Yokohl Valley Ranch where we stayed with Harvey and Bobbie for a week, before returning to the UK.

It was good to see the ranch for our second time and Harvey drove us round in his 4WD. The pastures, as on our previous visit, were extremely brown, but the cattle all looked fit and well. Although Harvey was by now fully retired from managing the ranch, he remained as consultant and was to have the occupancy of the ranch house for life.

The owner of the ranch lives in the state of Idaho and has many interests other than the cattle ranch. One of his main enterprises is cotton growing in Tulare County in mid-California. Harvey and Marty, the present ranch manager, took Mary and I for a full day's visit to this vast estate. It covers 250,000 acres of dead flat land which was fully reclaimed from Lake Tulare in the early 20th century. It is divided into 640 acre sections, with water channels surrounding each section for irrigating the land with the aid of powerful mobile pumps.

With not a tree or any other sign of vegetation in sight, a five-acre administration block surrounded with palm trees was a welcome sight from the rows and rows of white cotton. Also in this enclosure was the helicopter on its pad which was in constant use around the cotton fields. The harvesting of the crop was well underway with 96 picking machines, mostly driven by students during their summer vacation. These machines each stripped the heads off six rows of cotton which were elevated to an overhead tank. At the boundary of each section was a long metal tank into which the cotton was deposited. It was then pressed into bales 30ft in length and eventually carted to the estate Cotton Gin. Early morning mist dictated the starting time of harvesting and, once started, it was kept up until nightfall.

To make sure that time-wasting was kept to a minimum, several mobile loos toured the cotton fields continuously, to service the mixed-sex labour force. Mobile canteens also toured the cotton fields, carrying instant meals which I believe the drivers ate on the move.

Since our previous visit to the ranch a sand-based, equine arena had been developed for the use of the staff and their children. The main sport was 'steer roping' which is quite an exciting spectacle to watch. For our parting gift we were honoured with a special display of this very popular pastime.

Mary and Stan, home on the range in the Yokohl Valley, Central California

14. From Sickness To Stardom

A few weeks after our return from the USA I was diagnosed with quite a serious heart problem and was admitted to Guys Hospital just after Christmas 1993. The heart surgeon advised that I should have an immediate operation for the replacement of the aortic valve. He gave me the choice of a plastic valve or a pig's tissue valve, but strongly advised me to have the latter, which I duly did.

At the time of my admission to Stephen Ward in Guys Hospital, a serious flu epidemic had broken out and many of the intensive care nurses were stricken with it and unable to carry out their duties. As a result of this situation I had to wait 13 days for my operation. The surgeon told me that I was not fit to be sent home but must remain in hospital and hope for the best.

My wait, although frustrating, was made bearable with the help of my bed neighbour, Brian Dron. After an introductory chat we formed a friendship that was kept up until our operations, which were similar, and still exists to this day with Mary and I meeting Brian and his wife Angela on some occasion each year.

With a bit of good luck Brian had got a Scrabble set with him and challenged me to a game, which I immediately accepted. Now Brian, who was a retired headmaster thought it would be a walkover against a village schoolboy-cum-farmer but, after playing 37 games during the 13-day wait, he was the winner by only two games. A considerable amount of interest was shown in us two old boys sitting in the space between the beds, with plenty of tips forthcoming from over-enthusiastic observers. Each day one of the doctors called to watch our state of play on his morning round of the ward. One morning he congratulated both of us for finding such an interesting game to while away the time, and wished a few more of the patients would follow suit.

Eventually, we both went to the operating theatre on the same morning but, after coming out of intensive care 48 hours later, neither of us gave much thought to Scrabble. The very kindly nurse who was caring for me asked, as I became half-awake, if there was anything I fancied to eat or drink. I can just remember saying, "Please, could you get me a low-fat, fruit yoghurt." In what seemed next to no time, she handed me the most welcome black cherry yoghurt, the best I had ever tasted - and she spoon-fed me with it!

Although Stephen Ward was rather outdated and parts of it needed a lick of paint, the nurses were friendly and helpful, with over 30 beds to attend. The pay telephone on the ward had been out of order for some time, but calls could be made without payment, with the result that it was being exploited to the full, with relatives and friends receiving calls that were free and unexpected.

One rather amusing incident occurred on the morning I was going down for my operation. It was a strict rule that every patient had to have a complete bath, pre-op. I had finished mine and was on the point of letting the water out when a very elderly gentleman asked me to leave the water in for his bath. I told him that this wasn't permissible under the hygiene rules, but his reply to this was that he only had a bath once monthly and thought it a complete waste of water to use it just the once. The nurse in charge, hearing this discussion, came and gently persuaded him to do as he was told.

My operation was a success and about seven years ago I had a request from Dr Fox, a consultant from the William Harvey Hospital in Ashford, asking me if I would take part in a weekend hospital training course that he organised at three monthly intervals. The reason he made this request was the fact that I had successfully had a pig's tissue aortic valve replacement and would fit into his team of medical guinea pigs.

I usually attend the 8.30am session on Saturdays which concludes at 1.00pm, though it is often much later. On entry into the outpatients' section I am delegated to a vacant consulting room, complete with my name on the entrance door. I clad myself in a dressing gown, ready to be examined by the trainee doctors who, may I add, come from all parts of the world. When I started on this exercise the examining doctor would enter the room, along with four or five of his trainees who would in turn give me a thorough examination. With this task completed the examiner would question each one in turn and ask them for their diagnosis. The answers to my heart condition varied quite considerably, but mostly they were reasonably correct.

The order of examination has now changed with each trainee coming into the room individually and reporting to the examiner in his office with his or her findings. I find this routine tiring, after approximately 30 trainees have each asked me to lay on the bed and present my body for their investigation. At the end of each session I feel that I have been of some use to the medical profession that a few years ago was able to give me an extended lease of life.

A couple of months after my return from Guys, Mary and I got involved in an exciting session of filming, the cause of which was the Armstrong car. It had now been in the family for 60 years, having recovered from its road accident on our Scottish holiday in 1969. After a lot of heart-searching and discussion within the family it was decided that it was time to sell it. Mary's brother Tom had carefully carried out a lot of maintenance work on it over a good many years and, thanks to him, it was in very good order, both mechanically and visually.

At that time, one of our regular customers at the farm shop was Jenny Ballo, a reporter from the *Kentish Express* and on hearing our intention to sell the Armstrong, the car that she often admired, she suggested that she contact the Southern ITV news team. A few days later they arrived at the farm and Mary drove the car around the quiet lane surrounding the farm and was interviewed whilst driving. The very next evening she found herself as one of the highlights on the Southern TV news, driving her 60-year-old car around this very rural setting.

One thing leads to another and within a few days we had a phone call from the BBC asking if we would care to take the car to London to take part in *Treasure Hunt*, a television programme hosted by Anneka Rice. The BBC offered to arrange transport and meet the cost. To this we agreed and a few days later this transport arrived and conveyed Mary and I, along with the car, to London. On arrival I drove the car up quite a steep ramp onto the roof of Whiteley's store where the broadcast was to take place.

After a short while Anneka welcomed us and was very impressed to have such an attractive old car to show off on her *Treasure Hunt*. Mary was delighted to answer the many questions that she was asked about the life of the car and was given a big thank you from Anneka at the end of the show.

The next episode in our newly acquired stardom took place alongside the River Mersey in Liverpool. The evening before our meeting with Anneka we had an urgent call from Carlton Television, requesting our company on their show *This Morning* with Richard and Judy. After explaining that we were being filmed by the BBC the next morning, they suggested they arrange transport to collect the car from Whiteley's and that Mary and I travel 1st class rail to Liverpool, our fares to be refunded. On arrival we were met by taxi and driven to a hotel near to the television broadcasting site where we were booked in for a two-night stay. The following morning before the show we both had to attend the make-up parlour where I spent a very embarrassing 40 minutes having various odd shades of cream applied to my face and neck, and gently massaged into my skin. Never in my life had I envisaged such a sissy act being applied to my body!

After quite a lengthy interview with Richard and Judy we were thanked for coming along and asked if we would like a tour of the city in one of their taxis, to which we readily agreed.

The following morning the car was loaded onto the transport and taken back to Kent. Mary and I were presented with £100, taken to Manchester Airport and given a 1st class ticket to Gatwick, where a taxi was waiting to take us home to Biddenden.

The car had been entered into a sale at the Weald of Kent Golf Club and created quite a bit of interest, including phone calls from a member of the Armstrong family who resided in Canada. It reached the sum of £10,500 in the auction, 18 times its cost in 1935.

Mary at the wheel of the Armstrong Siddeley 17hp touring saloon

15. Down Memory Lane

Recently Rosemary and Mary started a search into the family history of the Lane and the Gittins families (my mother's family). Through various channels they gleaned a lot of interesting information and, as a result of these findings, they decided that they would like to make a trip to Herefordshire and Worcestershire to look up some of the places where our relatives lived and the places of their burial.

One day, early in June 2005, for the first time in 36 years, Mary, Rosemary, Margaret and myself set off on a short family holiday, which turned out to be a very enjoyable and informative one. With a 5.00am start we arrived in Worcester at 9.30am just as the County Record Office was opening. Margaret and I were admitted right away after security checks, leaving Mary and Rosemary to continue onto the County Archives where an appointment had been made for a search. The staff in the Record Office were very helpful for the full three hours that we stayed there. Lots of very large volumes of records were produced for us to study at will.

The three most interesting documents traced the lifespan of Stanford-on-Teme School from 1889 until its closure in 1950. For almost every term day of that period the Headmaster had entered notes. All of my brothers and sisters had been to the school during that period, with my time there stretching from 1928-1935 when my youngest sister and I moved to Abbeydore.

Reading through these books brought back memories of many boys and girls who I had forgotten about, but when any of them were included in the daily notes I quickly saw them as long-lost school friends.

The Lane family had several mentions and I was glad not to see any adverse comments about them. One reference to me was made on 7th January 1932, on the orders of the district nurse: "Stanley Lane must not attend school until he is clear of ringworms on his neck and body." I remember vividly those three weeks when I was kept at home. It was a period of hard frost, and Father and brother Syd were coppicing an area of woodland surrounding a pond in one of the fields at the top end of the farm. As some of the light timber fell onto the frozen pond my job was to drag it out onto the adjoining bank where a fire was kept on the go. I enjoyed these weeks away from school and was quite disappointed when the district nurse visited me one day and told Mother she considered me safe to go back to school as the ringworms were cured.

Stanford was in the heart of the hop-growing district of the Teme Valley and the school holidays were always in the month of September to coincide with the hop picking. Most of the children took part and, until his death, Mr Routledge the headmaster, did some of the measuring. One entry in the school book made a note to the effect that the harvesting of the hop crop that year was rather drawn out as a result of bad weather conditions, and that the holiday was to be extended for one week to enable the crop to be cleared. I wonder how a situation similar to this would pass the books today!

Margaret was most intrigued with the various references entered into these books and had quite a chuckle comparing them to the present-day record books to which she has access in her work as a school teacher.

Another interesting entry was at the final closing of the school in 1950; the attendance of the final year had been only 29 children and the daily average for the whole school life was 35 children.

Rosemary and Mary had an informative session at the County Archives, after which they picked up Margaret and I, and we proceeded to Sale Green Farm to have lunch with Felicity and Andrew Bomford and my late brother, Arthur's widow, Bea. We had a good, long chat with farming being much the main topic.

From there we had a look at Cheltry Cottage in Stanford-on-Teme where I had lived for a year after leaving Adams Wood Farm in 1935. Nearly half a mile before reaching the cottage, I pointed out the well in the forecourt of The Green, a large country residence from which the owner had given Mother permission to draw our drinking water. The water at the cottage had been condemned. I used to draw two buckets full each morning for the family daily use, but I don't think I would relish the job today! We stayed and had a peep at the old water mill alongside the River Teme, where we children spent many happy hours playing in its dilapidated state - now restored to a superior residence.

Next stop was Stanford School which is now being used as the village hall since its closure in 1950. The building, which is built of red brick, is in very good condition and it was good to look through the windows to get a glimpse of both the classrooms where I had sat all those years ago. It brought back so many memories of my days in this small school.

Stanford Church, where both of my parents are buried, with the ashes of my sister, Edith, was in a state of major repair work and was locked up, much to our disappointment. The two headstones are still in quite good condition after 70 years.

Adams Wood Farm was our next stop which we viewed from the entrance off Poke Lane. Sadly, the lovely old house and buildings have been converted into three separate dwellings, plus an old outlying cattle yard and barn at the further part of the farm has now become a luxury dwelling.

On our arrival in Presteigne sister Jennie and Ernie welcomed us for a three-night stay, while Rosemary and Margaret went on to their cousins Tony and Pat in Eardisley.

The following morning Rosemary and Margaret had an appointment at the County Archives in Hereford which they found of great interest. Thursday afternoon was taken up with a visit to my cousin Jean and husband Brian who live in a very picturesque valley near to Builth Wells in mid-Wales. Jean is my youngest cousin and also the youngest granddaughter of Grandmother Gittins, who was blessed with a total of 39. Quite a few of them I never had the pleasure of getting to know. There are just five who I know of left at this present time. We spent several hours chatting about various cousins and their lives, before we left Jean and Brian in peace, having tried to build a family network.

The next morning Rosemary and Margaret picked Mary and I up from Jennie's and we spent a very interesting day touring round some places with family ties. First we called at Middleton-on-the-Hill Church and found several family graves of the Gittins family and were lucky to find the very neat church open.

I remember as a young boy Mother telling us that her sister Annie Oliver had bequeathed in her will a sum of money to pay for a new organ to be fitted in the Church. It gave me pleasure to read the plaque on the front of the organ stating that in 1930 this organ had been installed from a legacy of the late Annie Oliver who died in 1929. She had no children of her own but had brought up two nephews who had been orphaned at the death of her sister at an early age.

Our next call was at the Ford Farm in the same parish. This is the farm where Mother and her 12 brothers and sisters were born. Grandfather Gittins had moved there from Shropshire in 1871. I will not dwell too much on the farm as I have already mentioned it in previous pages. The house and buildings looked in well-kept condition. Mrs Price, the owner's wife, invited us to join her for a cup of tea which enabled us to hear a little bit about her time at the Ford which they had occupied for 50 years.

The next place of call was at Upton Court in the parish of Leysters. This was the home of the Lane family from 1705 until 1887, the year when my Father was born. The house, which dates back to Elizabethan times, is now in a very bad state and quite depressing to look at. The fine old buildings are much the same, so sad.

Our lengthy search in nearby Little Hereford churchyard for the grave of my grandmother, Jane Lane, who was buried there in 1887 proved fruitless, much to our disappointment and that of four pairs of wet feet searching in the long grass.

We then carried on through Tenbury Wells towards Bromyard, calling at Lower Underly Farm, the birthplace of my grandmother. This farm is of considerable size and had recently changed hands, not a soul in sight apart from a big group of Friesian calves lying in the corner of a field close by a tidy set of farm buildings.

The Golden Valley was our next destination. This valley, with its profusion of daffodils each spring, runs the entire length of the River Dore from its source in the foothills of the Black Mountains until it joins the River Monnow at Pontrilas. We called at Ewyas Harold and had a peep at the school where I spent the last term of my school life and found that it had been closed since 1963, and is now the village hall. Further up the valley we stopped in the village of Abbeydore where I had lived from 1935 till 1937. The Abbey where I had attended services and Sunday school is in immaculate condition, but the school which I had attended has been closed since 1958, and is now used as the village hall. Walking by the schoolyard we got into conversation with a man about the village and, hearing the name Lane, he got quite excited.

His wife's father had bought Bryn-Y-Nant, the house that they lived in, from Mother in 1938. We were all invited to call in and have a cup of tea with him and his wife. The garden that I had looked after as a boy is now a showpiece. They had spent a lot of time and, I suspect, a lot of money to make it such. They brought me up-to-date with much of the life that has existed there during the 68 years since I left the village.

Friday we set off back home after a lovely break. Our last place of call was to the Church at Wolferlow which, sadly, is now permanently closed. We searched the churchyard for the grave of my great-grandmother, Jane Baldwin, but alas, to no avail.

As we were sitting in the car alongside of the churchyard, which is situated in a very isolated, but picturesque part of the countryside, a car pulled up and an elderly man got out, obviously keen to have a chat. On hearing that I was born in the neighbouring parish of Upper Sapey we had a long chat and, just before wishing him farewell, he told us his name, John Thacker. He produced a tape that he had composed about his life as a farmer. We bought the three-hour tape and have found it of great interest, as he mentions several people who I remember from my childhood all those years ago, including Dr Russell, who removed the wart from my knee, way back in 1932!

*

As I am now about to conclude my journal I would like to say how thankful I am to all the folk who have helped to make this, my life, such a happy one. Although I am now semi-retired from the farm I still take a close interest in all the activities and undertake a few light tasks, which I am sure are appreciated by both Rosemary and Mike. My favourite, early-morning job is driving around in the farm truck and 'lookering' (the Kentish name for attending to outlying livestock) a certain amount of sheep and young cattle in different pastures around the farm. I must admit that I am a little bit slow getting around, but what does it matter - the day is all my own, and the bacon butty that Mary always has waiting for me on my return to breakfast, is enjoyed with relish. It gives me great pleasure to be able to drive around the farm and keep up-to-date with all that is going on. It is nearly devoid of docks, but just a few thistles await a visit from Rosemary on the quad bike with a knapsack sprayer on her back!

Other members of the family are also flourishing. Margaret and Shaun still enjoy the variety offered by their day-to-day work as school teachers, although they, along with most teachers, are finding the profession under increasing pressure from bureaucracy.

Miriam has just completed a course in Fine Art at West Kent College in Tonbridge and is now taking a year off before starting a degree course in Illustration. Lydia will be taking her GCSEs and still enjoys dancing. Alice has just completed her second year of a six-year degree course in veterinary medicine at Cambridge with a good pass rate, and is currently odd-jobbing during her summer break. Peter works fulltime on the farm during his summer break and is currently at Harper Adams Agriculture College for the final year of his degree course.

A number of my relatives are still farming in various parts of the country; some I keep in touch with, but having so many cousins whose parents were farming, I seem to have lost touch with others.

In recent years Mary and I have joined a team of Welcomers at All Saints Church, Biddenden. From early April 'til mid-October we undertake a two-hour duty each Thursday. Mary usually leaves this little job to me, but always steps in if I have other commitments. The visitors are met at the Church entrance and, after a few words of welcome, are given a brief guide to the building and offered a guide board to take around with them. These boards are written in either English, French, German or Dutch, and serve the needs of most of our visitors. We also get many visitors from other parts of the world, some of whom are ancestor-hunting. A few of them spend a considerable time browsing around the many grave stones with the hope that they may find some reference to their family.

One of the more senior members of our parish, Jack Withereden, is always willing to help with their enquiries and has derived much pleasure in tracing many of their relatives. I often get asked about local eating places and B&B accommodation. On one occasion a Dutch cycling couple were looking for a nice, quiet spot where they could pitch their tent for the night. I invited them back to the farm, where they spent two nights camped in a field which was occupied by a large number of lambs that had just been weaned. In spite of the lambs being rather vocal in their enforced absence from their mothers, the visitors were so pleased to have spent two nights on a farm site, so close to nature.

Some days the numbers are very small and I revert to reading passages from the Bible to while away the time, a practice that I remember being very keen on during my Sunday school days.

One of my other interests is helping Mary in her garden, but being very careful not to put a foot in the wrong place or pull up a flower in mistake for a weed! The vegetable garden is my domain and I endeavour to keep both families supplied with fresh vegetables the whole year round. Occasionally, Margaret and family are able to share some of them during the most productive season which is usually from early July to mid-November, with runner beans being top of the league. I find it disappointing that so few people grow vegetables in their gardens now, unlike in my younger days, when most country dwellers kept a well-stocked kitchen garden. Some of them support our own growers, but far too many of them seem quite happy to buy produce that has to be transported many thousands of miles from faraway countries. Most of it could be grown quite easily on the many thousands of acres that are today being classed as 'set aside' and which are not contributing anything whatsoever to the national larder.

I still like to attend Ashford Market from time to time, to keep up with trends and have a chance to meet some other farmers, many of whom I have known for over half a century. Looking back all those years reminds me of the local sheep and cattle fairs that were held at different times of the year. Most of them were just one day fairs, with the exception of Biddenden which stretched to two days, sheep on the first Wednesday in November and cattle on the following day. Tenterden held two sheep fairs, one in May and one in September. Benenden held its fair in May and Northland, if my memory serves me correctly, in late August.

The last of the sheep fairs to survive was in Horsmonden which was held during the last week in July in a field just outside the village. It was discontinued following the serious outbreak of foot and mouth disease that struck the country in 2001. We got off very lightly compared to the stricken areas in the north of the country. With our land being rather scattered within a radius of about three miles and our lambing coming in the midst of the outbreak, we had to change our grazing pattern for the season to conform with the MAFF restriction on livestock movements.

All the ewes were housed at White House Farm at the time of the outbreak and at lambing, instead of taking the ewes and lambs to the outlying pastures for the summer, we had to keep then on the home farm. We made silage on those fields away from home, and grazed the pastures that were usually reserved for conservation - a practice we hope never to repeat.

*

I can now look back on all of those happy years that I have spent in the farming world, with just a break of four and a half years serving in the Royal Navy during the Second World War. So many changes have taken place during those years. From the depression farming years of the 1930s to the outbreak of WW2 in 1939 came the urgent call to the nation to produce as much food as possible from our own farms. This plea was answered with much enthusiasm from the farming community, alongside members of the general public in their various walks of life. It makes me feel proud to have shared in such a vital period of our national history. Our citizens seem to excel themselves in times of national crisis, long may this patriotism remain.

At the present time the politicians of the day look on farmers as a bit of a pest and do their utmost to make themselves out to know just what path we should be taking in the near future: so many rules and regulations being imposed on us by the powers in Brussels, and the UK the only member state to adhere to them.

Just now, in the first decade of the 21st century, farming in this country is being run down at an alarming rate, with the result that few of the younger generation are willing to face the uncertain future of the industry.

To the young men and women who are brave enough to venture out into this hazy future I offer my heartfelt wishes for the success I am sure that they will achieve, and hope they will appreciate that they have chosen the most important profession of all, that of helping produce food for mankind the world over.

Above: Adams Wood Farm in 1992. Below: Stan and Mary at Stanford-On-Teme School in 2005. It closed in 1950 and is now the village hall

Sketch of Stan by Miriam Small, his granddaughter, in 2003